Computer Upgrades
Made Easy

Computer Upgrades Made Easy

Walter Bragg

Writers Club Press
New York Lincoln Shanghai

Computer Upgrades Made Easy

Writers Club Press
an imprint of iUniverse, Inc.

For information address:
iUniverse, Inc.
2021 Pine Lake Road, Suite 100
Lincoln, NE 68512
www.iuniverse.com

Author's Contact Information:
Beckley, West Virginia
Bragg_walter@hotmail.com
http://shotguns.vstorecomputers.com

ISBN: 0-595-26483-2

Printed in the United States of America

I want to thank my loving wife, Faith. Who has given support and understanding thought out our happy marriage.

In addition, I her would like to thank my father, Walter and my mother, Jackie for their love and support.

And especially my son Gene. Who was my biggest supporter and My proof reader. Thanks

Contents

CHAPTER 1   Get to know your computer and parts 1

CHAPTER 2   Getting to know DOS 7

CHAPTER 3   18 Common Problems That Your Plague Your
Computer 13

CHAPTER 4   How to Diagnose Case Problems 28

CHAPTER 5   Diagnosing PC Hardware Problems 32

CHAPTER 6   ScanDisk and Defragmenter 35

CHAPTER 7   How To: Install a Printer 37

CHAPTER 8   Removing and replacing the battery 41

CHAPTER 9   What is cache memory? 43

CHAPTER 10   All about RAM and How to Add RAM 45

CHAPTER 11   How to Install a Internal Modem 50

CHAPTER 12   How to connect an external modem 52

CHAPTER 13   The Floppy Drive and What is does 54

CHAPTER 14   Video cards 101 58

CHAPTER 15   Install a Sound Card 61

CHAPTER 16   CD-ROM and how to install 64

CHAPTER 17   DVD upgrade 70

CHAPTER 18   How do you install a Zip drive and use it? 75

CHAPTER 19   How do I install dual Video cards? 78

CHAPTER 20   Raid 80

CHAPTER 21   How to install a hard drive 86

CHAPTER 22   How to partition your Hard Drive 94

CHAPTER 23   How to Install a New CPU. 102

CHAPTER 24   The Cooling Fan. 104

CHAPTER 25   Install power a new supply 106

CHAPTER 26   How to Identify Chips on the
                   Motherboard. 108

CHAPTER 27   Install a New Motherboard. 111

CHAPTER 28   Building the new PC. 113

CHAPTER 29   How to Reprogram your Computer 144

CHAPTER 30   Miscellaneous 146

1

Get to know your computer and parts

First you need to get to know your computer and its parts. Getting to know to the parts will help you make the upgrades later on. A personal computer is made up of many components; called hardware. This article briefly explains each hardware component in turn.

A typical PC contains the following hardware:

Case Power Supply Motherboard

CPU Memory Hard Disk

Floppy Disk CD-ROM Video Adapter

Sound Card Modem Mouse

Keyboard

There are many other possible hardware components, such as a DVD, CD-RW, Zip drive or network card. There are also many sub components of a PC, such as the cooling fan, printer port or reset switch to name a few. This article focuses on the basic PC hardware. The hardware in the list above is nearly universal to a basic PC.

While a PC is built up from hardware components, the hardware is only half of the equation. The other vital part of a PC is the software. Without software, the hardware is useless; and vice versa.

The fundamental software for a PC is called an operating system. Without an operating system or OS, a PC can't do much! The operating system tells the components of a PC what to do and when to do it. Windows, MAC OS, Linux and UNIX are all examples of operating systems.

The case is the box that houses the PC. All of the hardware, except for the peripherals, is housed inside case. There are two common styles of cases: desktop and tower. The desktop case usually sits under the monitor and is roughly the size of two or three shoe boxes side by side. The tower case stands upright on one end and is usually placed on the floor. Tower cases can be the same size as a desktop case but often range up much larger. Another, less common, case style is the rack mount case which slides in and out of an equipment rack.

Where the power cord connects to the back of the PC is the power supply. The power supply converts AC current from the wall outlet to the appropriate DC voltages for the various components of the computer.

The power supply has a fan built into it to keep itself and the PC cool. Most PC's have at least one additional cooling fan, often mounted directly on the CPU. The power supply or its internal fan can wear out. Fortunately, the entire unit is easily replaced.

The motherboard is the largest and most fundamental component of a PC. Every other hardware component is somehow attached to the motherboard. The motherboard is the common link for every component to communicate and work together.

The motherboard has a series of slots, sockets and connectors for connecting the various components of a PC. The memory, accessory cards, and CPU are installed directly onto the motherboard in most cases. The drives and peripherals communicate with the motherboard through wired connections.

It is becoming increasingly common for motherboards to integrate features that used to require separate accessory cards. Most motherboards integrate drive controllers and communication ports; and with greater frequency they integrate sound, video and network features as well.

There are wide ranges of motherboards to choose from. They differ in features, speed, capacity and the CPU supported. They also differ in size, shape and layout; this is commonly referred to as the form factor.

The CPU, which stands for Central Processing Unit, is the brain of the PC. It is often referred to as the processor or chip. The CPU directs coordinates and communicates with the hardware components and performs all of the thinking. What a CPU actually does is perform mathematical calculations. It is the software that people write that translates those calculations into useful functions for us.

The speed of the CPU, generally speaking, is the number of calculations it can perform in one second. It is more complicated than that, but it is a reasonable way to think of the speed. A 500 MHz (megahertz) CPU performs about 500,000,000 mathematical calculations per second.

As the speed of new CPUs increase, the difference is becoming less obvious to computer users. A CPU that is twice as fast as another one will not result in a PC running twice as fast. The CPU has to wait for other, slower components and for the user too. The CPU spends a lot of time sitting idle, waiting for something to do.

CPU's has something called a cache or memory cache. The memory cache is where information is stored that the CPU is likely to need soon. This memory is in addition to the normal memory installed in a PC. The difference is that the cache is built right onto the CPU (and/ or very near the CPU), and it is much faster than conventional memory. Cache memory was developed to reduce the time the CPU had to wait while information was retrieved from the standard memory.

The memory chips store information, temporarily, for short term use. A PC's memory is an entirely different thing from the hard disk memory. The hard disk stores information permanently for long term use.

A PC's memory only contains information when the PC is on. When the PC is turned off, the information in the memory chips disappears. The information in memory is similar to a thought, it gets replaced when you start thinking about something else. Hard disk memory is like writing down the information and storing it in a filing cabinet.

The floppy disk drive is a device that records data onto a removable storage disk called a floppy disk. Floppy disks, also called floppies, are the most basic storage medium for data. However their limited capacity, typically 1.44 megabytes, makes them of limited use. A floppy disk can be used to copy files from one PC to another PC or for making backup copies of files. Replacing a floppy drive is very easy and inexpensive to do, should the need arise.

The CD-ROM drive is a device that reads information or music off of a compact disk (CD). CD-ROM stands for Compact Disc Read Only Memory. Most software is distributed on CDs because of their low cost and large capacity (650MB or more).

The CD is spun at high speed inside the drive while a laser is directed at the surface to read the data or music. The CD-ROM speed is referenced as 12X or 12 speed (or any other number). This simply means that it spins the CD that many times faster than the original industry specification. So, a 48X CD-ROM spins the CD up to 48 times faster than the original specification. Faster is better.

Many PCs are now built with a CD-RW drive, which stands for Compact Disc, Read-Write. Unlike a standard CD-ROM, you can write data onto a CD with a CD-RW drive. CD-R disks allow you to write to the CD once and read it an unlimited number of times. With the use of RE-writable CDs(CD-RW's) you can reuse the disk and rewrite over it again many times.

The speeds of a CD-RW are expressed like this, 4X 8X 32X. This means it can write to the CD up to 4 times the spec speed, rewrite the CD up to 4 times spec speed and read the CD up to 32 times the spec speed The video adapter card or graphics adapter translates information into graphics and text that appear on the monitor screen.

The graphics adapter plugs into a slot on the motherboard or is incorporated directly into the electronics of the motherboard. Most motherboards now include a slot specifically designed for the graphics adapter called the AGP slot (Advanced Graphics Port). Modern graphics adapters usually incorporate some memory right on the card to improve their performance. To further improve the performance of the video output, a second graphics accelerator card can be used in tandem with the graphics adapter.

The Parts of a Personal Computer-

The Sound Card How-To > PC > Overview

Most PCs are typically equipped for multimedia. They can play sounds, music, and speech. The sound card processes the information and outputs the signal to the speakers.

The sound card plugs into a slot on the motherboard or is incorporated directly into the motherboard. With a basic sound card a microphone, speakers, joystick and an auxiliary sound source can be connected to it. More advanced cards may offer additional input and output features.

The modem is a device that enables the PC to use a telephone line to communicate with other PCs and devices. The name comes from Modulation Demodulator. The modem plugs into a slot on the motherboard or is incorporated directly into the electronics of the motherboard. It converts data into signals that can be transmitted over the telephone line and receives data to convert back for the PC to use.

The mouse is a user input device that enables you to communicate with your PC. By moving the mouse and pressing the two or three buttons, you can highlight and select images on the screen to give directions to your PC. Some mice offer a wheel to aid in the scrolling of a window without having to move the mouse.

A wire usually connects a mouse but wireless mice are also available. Wired mice may use a serial, PS/2 or a USB port. Other variations of mice available include the trackball and touch pad.

The mouse detects movement either as a ball underneath the mouse rolls along your desk or by using a light inside the mouse and measuring the reflection from the desktop. The mouse is a user-input device that enables you to communicate with your PC. By moving the mouse and pressing the two or three buttons, you can highlight and select images on the screen to give directions to your PC. Some mice offer a wheel to aid in the scrolling of a window without having to move the mouse. A wire usually connects a mouse but wireless mice are also available. Wired mice may use a serial, PS/2 or a USB port. Other variations of mice available include the trackball and touch pad. The mouse detects movement either as a ball underneath the mouse rolls along your desk or by using a light inside the mouse and measuring the reflection from the desktop.

2

Getting to know DOS

We've all been there, fuming, as our computer pummels us with meaningless error messages, beeps, and blips.

Was it the new antivirus you just installed? The virtual plant you downloaded that grows if you water It and shrivels if you don't? Who knows what it could be, but there is a tool to help troubleshoot your problems.

Start troubleshooting

Open msconfig by going to Start, choosing Run (or hit the Windows key+R), and typing "msconfig" without the quotes. You can learn more about how to open msconfig and some of its other uses here.

Below the list of services, check the box titled "Hide All Microsoft Services." Microsoft's default services will disappear and you will be left with those of foreign parties. Third-party services are necessary, especially for antivirus software, but you can temporarily uncheck Services to see if a certain application is the culprit in your Windows woes.

Remember to recheck the services when you are finished troubleshooting, as some of your applications will need them to function properly.

You can open a Windows Explorer window from within DOS by typing, "start." without the quotes (that's "start" followed by a space and a period). An Explorer window will open starting from the folder you are in.

If you type "start…" (that's "start" followed by a space and two periods) without the quotes, you'll open the folder above the folder you are in. This works in all versions of Windows.

Bonus: A couple more great uses for the period and the double period: If you go to Start—> Run and type a period you will open an Explorer window to your desktop folder. If you type two periods, you guessed it; you open an Explorer window to the folder directly above your desktop.

MSCDEX stands for Microsoft CD Extensions. This file allows your operating system to talk to your CD-ROM drive.

CD-ROMs file information differently than your hard drive does. Because Microsoft designed DOS and Windows 3.1 before CD drives became common, they need special instructions in order to read-and-write—CD-ROM data. Windows 95,98, ME and XP which came out after CDs became popular, have these instructions built in. You'll need to follow these steps to teach your older OS to work with CDs. Don't worry; we'll go into each step in detail in the next few pages.

Find the DOS driver, also called the "real-mode" driver, for your particular CD ROM drive.

Install the driver.

Edit the config.sys file to add the information about your CD type.

Edit the autoexec.bat file to point to the newly installed driver.

Before your computer can recognize your CD-ROM drive, it needs a driver to show it the way. You will find this file on the original installation disk that came with your CD drive. If you've lost the disk, try the drive manufacturer's website, or stop by **www.windrivers.com** and search for the brand name and model of your CD drive.

When you find the driver, download it to your computer and install it.

Part 2: Edit config.sys

Editing your config.sys file is not as scary as it sounds. All you're doing is telling this file where it can find the driver for your CD-ROM drive.

Use the Find command in the Start Menu to locate your config.sys file. Before you do anything else, make a copy of config.sys onto a floppy disk. (You never can be too careful.)

Open the config.sys file on your hard drive and look for a line that begins:

Device=

Plug in the name of your CD-ROM driver, like this:

Device=atapi_CD.sys

You also need to tell config.sys to look for the CD somewhere other than on your hard drive. You thus assign your CD drive a letter and a name. Let's assign it to Drive D, and name it MSCD001 (which is often the default.)

Device=atapi_CD.sys/D:MSCD001

You're almost done. The config.sys file now knows where to find your CD-ROM driver and what to call it. It's time to let your Microsoft extensions know as well.

Make a copy of autoexec.bat onto a floppy before you open it.

Now open autoexec.bat on your hard drive. You want this file to launch MSCDEX.exe at startup and to point to the newly installed CD driver. All you need to do is add this line to the file:

C:\windows\commands\MSCDEX.exe/D:MSCD001

Next time you restart your computer and launch DOS, the machine should be able to find your CD-ROM drive.

FDISK/MBR

Repairs the master boot record on your computer. It's a great last-ditch troubleshooting step to run before you totally reformat your machine. The Master Boot Record usually resides on the first sector of your hard drive. The program begins the boot process by looking up the partition table to determine which partition to use for booting. It then transfers program control to the boot sector of that partition, which continues the boot process. That's why it's a particularly nasty place for viruses—it loads every time you boot your computer, and controls what boots where.

If you kill your MBR, your machine won't know what to do with itself. FDISK/status will give you the partition information of your drive.

ATTRIB

Sets or displays the attributes for your files. Type in ATTRIB with the following switches:

-r read/write

+r read only (if you want to delete a file, you must first make it read/write)

+h makes hidden file

-h reveals hidden file

+a archives the file—makes it available for archiving when using BACKUP or XCOPY

-a removes archiving

+s sets system attribute—marks the file as a command file used only by DOS

-s turns off system attribute

/s sets attributes on subdirectories found within the specified path.

Part 3: switches

FORMAT (including switches/s,/q,/u)

A lot of people make a crucial mistake when they format their hard drives—they leave it naked, without an operating system. Without an OS, your machine is just a bag of bolts with electrical current running through it.

The switch/s formats and leaves the system on the disk./Q means "quick", do it fast. It's like doing a quick format on a floppy disk. It just erases the data without formatting one sector at a time./U eliminates the back out "undo" option, so you can't UNFORMAT your hard disk.

DELTREE

DELTREE is a great shortcut for deleting huge directories. Let's say you uninstalled a program but it left tiny little files in a big, complicated directory string: C:PROGRAM FILESLAME PROGRAM-SAVED FOLDERSEXTRA STUFF.

If you type DELTREE C:PROGRAM FILESLAME PROGRAM it'll remove the LAME PROGRAM directory and all its subdirectories AND everything in them. Nuke-o-rama!! DELTREE gives you a Y/N option to turn it off.

Because you're SURE what you're doing, type DELTREE with the switch/Y-deltree YES! Then it won't ask you to confirm.

MD make directory

RD remove directory

DIR/w show directory listing, wide on the screen so you can read it

Part 4: Why isn't DOS recognizing my mouse?

You need a dual-boot machine, for starters. You can either use System Commander or add an older version of DOS as a boot option. The important part, though, is to make sure autoexec.dos and config.dos specify your CD-ROM and mouse drivers, so that DOS can find them.

Edit dosstart.bat in your Windows directory (or create one if it doesn't exist) and add the mouse command to it. The command will vary depending on the make and model of the mouse; for most Microsoft mice, it's C:/msinput/mouse.exe

3

18 Common Problems That Your Plague Your Computer

The three big COMPUTER killers are: 1. Static electricity, 2. Dirt and 3. Heat.

1. Static Electricity; is harmless to you but it can fry your computer chips. Static electricity is mainly caused by dry air and or friction e.g., dragging your feet across a carpet. It's best to use a grounding strip. Or touch the metal frame of your case to complete the ground before you unplug it. This does not work as well but it is better to be safe then sorry. To lower the risk of static electricity, avoid standing on carpet. Ideally, you should have your computer set up on a grounding mat. Consult your manual if you need help opening your computer's case.

2. Dirt; dust and dirt build up at an alarming rate on. Periodically pop the cover and wipe down the fans and vents power supplies, fan intakes and wherever there's controlled airflow. Over time, this build-up can choke your system to the point where it overheats and dies.

3. Heat; Keep your Computer at least six inches away from the wall or any thing else that could block the airflow around it. In addition, turn off you Computer when you are not using it for any length of time.

Hint When trouble does strike, eliminate the simplest and most obvious possibilities first. Make sure all cables, both internal and external, are in good condition and that all peripherals are plugged in and turned on.

Hardware problems

4.Windows can not find my hardware; Solution: Sometimes, Windows either fails to recognize new Plug-and-Play hardware or loses track of existing hardware after a crash or other problem. Check the manual to verify the device is installed correctly (plugged into the correct slot, powered on and so on). f that is not you're problems, right-click on My Computer and select Properties. Click on Device Manager and select the category and offending device (you may have to drill down a bit). If the device is flagged with a red X or yellow exclamation point, use the Properties button to see what's causing the problem e.g., a resource conflict.

If your hardware still won't work, click Remove. If Win98 asks to remove "files that are no longer needed" click yes, and do a full power-off reboot. When you restart, Windows should redetect the hardware you just removed and install the proper drivers (it may ask for the hardware's setup disk). If it does not, use the Add New Hardware wizard to select the device and its drivers manually.

I have found that on some Plug-and-Play hardware you have to remove the hardware from computer slot. Restart, install software, shout down the computer, and reinstall the hardware and restart Why this works I do not know but it does work when all else fails try this. In addition, remember always unplug your computer and plug the power back in last. It is better to be safe then sorry.

If even this fails, try the Web. Your problem could be an outdated driver, and you may find the answer in the support area or FAQ for that device.

5. My Plug-and-Play hardware still does not play; Solution: There's no doubt PnP has made upgrading easier. However, even PnP hardware can cause IRQ conflicts It's not uncommon for PnP not to detect or even to misname a new hardware, especially the first time around e.g.,

the first time to hook up your scanner the computer thinks it is a camera.

To give PnP a second chance, back up your hard disk and create an emergency boot diskette Next, follow the steps detailed in Problem No. 1 (Windows can not find my hardware). If this too fails, you may have to resolve an IRQ or I/O port conflict This can sometimes rescue an installation when all else fails. First, display Device Manager's hardware list, as before. Next, double-click a device's entry. Click the Resources tab and clear the Use Automatic Settings checkbox.

In the Resource Type list, double-click the IRQs, I/O ports and upper memory blocks (UMBs) Device Manager tell you conflict with other devices Then make new entries in the Edit Resource dialog. The dialog should restrict your choices to values your device supports, and advises you of any conflicts between the current resource assignments and those of other devices Once you've made your changes, click OK in all open dialogs and reboot.

Existing ISA cards can also cause conflicts, as can motherboard resources For example, your system BIOS may assign a Computer slot an IRQ that is already taken by an ISA card. If so, try turning off or reassigning motherboard resources through the BIOS. If your motherboard lets you use the BIOS to assign IRQs to Computer slots, this may also help you untangle things.

6. My SCSI scanner won't scan; Solution: Your adapter configuration may be at fault. Turn the Computer and scanner power off and all other external devices on. Physically remove the scanner from the external chain of SCSI or USB devices and make sure the last remaining device is properly terminated. If the scanner is the only external SCSI or USB device, connect a terminating plug to the external SCSI or USB connector.

If you have a camera and a scanner the Computer sometimes gets the too mixed up. Uninstall the camera and its software Reboot and try your scanner If your scanner works now you will only be able to use one or the other device on your computer, sorry.

Now reboot and make a note of the displayed SCSI ID numbers for whatever devices are still installed, and make sure all such devices-internal and external-are listed Turn off the Computer again and reconnect the scanner at the end of the external SCSI chain. Make sure the scanner is properly terminated, and if some other device in the chain was terminated previously, remove that termination. Be sure the scanner's SCSI ID number does not conflict with any number already in use, and don't use SCSI ID 7 (this is reserved for the internal SCSI host adapter).

Turn the scanner on, reboot and watch for a message to press Ctrl+A (or some other combination) to launch the host adapter configuration utility. Look for a SCSI Device Configuration option, select it and find the column that begins with the SCSI ID number assigned to the scanner. Change the Maximum Sync Transfer Rate to the lowest available number. While you are at it, change any options labeled Yes or Enabled to No or Disabled Save all changes, exit the utility, press any key to reboot and again watch the opening messages, which should now include the correct SCSI ID number for the scanner.

If Windows detects the scanner, it may prompt you for a vendor-supplied driver. If so, follow the vendor's directions for installing the software, reboot when prompted to do so, and when Windows restarts, go to Device Manager The scanner should now programmer in the list of devices under the Computer icon. Highlight it, click Properties and make sure no problems are listed. Exit Control Panel and run whatever diagnostic utilities came with the scanner.

7. My COMPUTER can not find by D drive; Solution: If you try to access your D: drive and Windows tells you that you do not have one,

or you see a drive listed that you know does not exist may have a CMOS problem the case of a missing diskette drive, open a DOS window and try to log onto that drive. If it's unavailable, run your Computer's CMOS configuration utility, usually by pressing the Delete key when prompted to do so during startup Make sure the status for each installed diskette drive is correct, then reboot You may be able to view the configuration from within a DOS window by pressing Ctrl+Alt+Enter or a similar key combination. This is handy for verifying the configuration, but you should make all changes from outside the Windows GUI, and follow up with a reboot.

Once all drives are available from a DOS command prompt, run Windows' Tweak UI program, select the My Computer tab and make sure all drive letters are checked Or, run RegEdit and open the following Registry key:

HKEY_CURRENT_USER1/4Software1/4Microsoft1/4Windows1/4CurrentVersion1/4Policies 1/4Explorer

If you see a No Drives entry, you should see either 00 00 00 00 or 0x00000000 (0) in its Data column, indicating no drives are disabled. If a nonzero value programmers, double-click the No Drives entry and change the values to all zeroes A disabled drive may cause odd side-effects, such as grayed-out Open and Explore options on the Start button's Context menu, so make sure all drives are enabled, even if you don't have a drive (B:) for example.

8. Windows Explorer keeps trying to read my floppy drive; Solution: A Registry setting is the likely culprit Run RegEdit, open the key listed in Problem No. 4 and check the No Drive Type Auto Run entry's Data column. If the first number is XY, where Y is hexadecimal 0, 1, 2, 3, 8, 9, A or B, Explorer will try to read all removable drives every time it opens. Change the number so that Y is 4, 5, C, D, E or F. Or, set it to 95, the Windows default. If that does not work, search the Registry's Data column for a:. If you find a reference to a:1/4filename.ext, some

active program may periodically try to find that file on the diskette drive Be on the lookout for a drive letter entry in any key whose name does not contain the initials MRU (for most-recently used). If you can locate the diskette with that file on it, uninstall and reinstall the program associated with that diskette Select its Custom option (if available) and rewrite all path options to point to locations on your hard drive. Check INI files, too, for references to a removable drive. If you are still using a CONFIG.SYS or AUTOEXEC.BAT file, make sure there's no PATH statement in either one that cites a removable drive letter.

Software problems

9. Windows won't wake up; Solution: Many consider this Win98's No. 1 shortcoming: After going into Suspend or Hibernation mode, the OS wakes up slowly or not at all. The problem results from subtle conflicts between Win98 and vendor-specific implementations of the Advanced Configuration and Power Interface (ACPI). In theory, if the hardware and BIOS are both ACPI compliant, power-saving Suspend and Hibernation modes will work fine with Win98, which also is ACPI compliant But theory and practice can be worlds apart.

Many systems now in use were designed for the older Advanced Power Management (APM) technology. They may require, at a minimum, a BIOS or driver update to work properly with the newer technology. Visit your hardware vendor's site to see what's required to make your system fully ACPI compliant.

Right click on the desktop any empty space will do. Click on properties that will open Display Properties Then click on Screen Saver and at bottom of the page click on Power. This will open the Power Options Properties Find system standby and or hibernate and option and select never, apply and close.

You may be able to turn off Advanced Power Management in your BIOS. When you start your computer watch the screen and follow the directions other hand, just look in the computer manual that came with your computer to get into your BIOS. In addition, look for Advanced Power Management if you have it turn it off.

10. Windows will not shut down; Solution: You should probably close all your programs yourself before you shut down Windows But if you let Windows close things down and you never make it to the "It's now safe to turn off your computer" message, there are two ways to fix things, depending on your symptoms:

If the hangs are intermittent, press Ctrl+Alt+Del when your system hangs to bring up the Close Program box. Some third-party programs, such as virus scanners, run in the background and can prevent your system from shutting down. First, try disabling the program If that does not work, uninstall it. If an item is flagged Not Responding, select it and click End Task. If that does not work, nor if nothing is flagged not Responding, try the Shut Down button. If that also fails, power off your system. Run ScanDisk when your reboot Try to notice patterns to your intermittent hangs. Is the same program or subsystem hanging? If so, check the vendor site for a patch or update.

If your system hangs every time, you are probably running Win98. Win98 uses a Fast Shutdown process whereby it sends a shutdown signal to all running programs and services, and then proceeds without waiting for a response. Some programs and subsystems respond too slowly or require an additional step before completely shutting down. This can foul up the shutdown sequence and result in a hang. The solution is to disable Fast Shutdown. To do that, run MSCON-FIG.EXE, click Advanced and check disable Fast Shutdown. Click OK twice and reboot. Win98 will now shut down in Win95's slower but sometimes fashion that is more reliable.

I have learned a trick. Rick click on an empty spot on your desktop/ new/shortcut. Then right click on properties on target line type AWINDOWS\RUNDLL.EXE user. exe, exit windows Athis will not work with Windows XP and Windows 2000. For windows XP and Windows 2000 use this. Rick click on an empty spot on your desktop/ new/shortcut. Then right click on properties on target line type ASHUTDOWN-S-t01"

11. System hangs at random intervals; Solution: Many things can contribute to intermittent problems, including defective RAM and unstable power supplies. Nevertheless, often-flaky drivers are to blame. In their haste to bring the latest and greatest hardware to market, many vendors take shortcuts in the device driver development and testing phase. The result is often a bug-ridden first-generation driver. Some vendors release hardware without drivers, forcing you to make do with older, often 16-bit DOS-based drivers.

To solve these problems, first back up your hard disk, then create an emergency boot diskette. If you are running Win95 be sure to place your CD-ROM driver and MSCDEX.EXE file on your diskette Win98's Emergency Boot Diskette Wizard adds these automatically. Next, check the Web site of your computer vendor, the device vendor or Microsoft for new drivers. The drivers that ship with hardware are seldom up to date. In almost all cases, you can find newer, less buggy versions.

Next, search your CONFIG.SYS file for DEVICE=lines that load 16-bit device drivers. These driver files usually have SYS extensions, but DRV or other extensions are also possible. If you find such a line, comment it out by inserting REM at the beginning of the line. Save the new CONFIG.SYS file and reboot. If all goes well, your computer may inform you it's found a new device, and ask you to insert your original Windows or hardware CD to obtain newer, 32-bit drivers. If your computer fails to boot, or a device no longer works correctly, you will have to restore the DEVICE=lines and reboot. It's then time to complain in earnest about the lack of proper drivers or purchase newer hardware with better driver support.

12. When I installed an program, another one suddenly stopped working; Solution: Your computer may have come down with a case of DLL Versions. DLLs (Dynamic Link Libraries) are disk files containing portions of programs. Breaking big programs into several parts allows each part to be loaded into RAM only when needed. In addition, several programs can simultaneously access the program snippets stored in a single DLL. This reduces the amount of disk space and RAM each program requires, and allows several programs to upgraded simultaneously by replacing a DLL they share.

Well-behaved installation programs place shared DLLs in the 1/4WINDOWS1/4SYSTEM directory, ensuring only one copy of a DLL resides on your hard disk. This not only saves disk space; it guarantees all programs use the same version of the DLL. But some setup programs create private copies of shared DLLs, so your hard disk may contain more than one version of a single DLL.

When a program executes a routine stored in a DLL, Windows first searches RAM for a previously loaded copy of the DLL. If that search fails, it searches your hard disk. As a result, if one program loads a private, out-of-date copy of a shared DLL, all programs running after that will use the private DLL because it's now in RAM. If these programs require a newer version of the DLL, they may crash or behave erratically.

To avoid this, make sure only one copy of each shared DLL resides on your hard disk. It should be the newest version, and should be in your 1/4WINDOWS1/4SYSTEM directory. Start with a utility like WDLLFnd (Treeless Software and Design, **http://members.aol.com/ TreeLessSW/wdllf2.htm**), which searches your hard disk for duplicate

DLLs. Right-click on each DLL's icon and select Properties to examine its file size and version information.

If all copies of a DLL are the same, move one copy to your 1/4WINDOWS1/4SYSTEM directory and delete the rest. If you have more than one version of a single DLL, save all older versions in a temporary hard disk directory or on a diskette and move the newest version to your 1/4WINDOWS1/4SYSTEM directory. Finally, reboot and test all programs.

13. Windows does not see all of my large hard drive; Solution: If you are using a large drive, you may need a new BIOS access method. Drives between 504MB and 8.4GB require a method known as Logical Block Addressing (LBA). Drives larger than that requires a revised LBA.

To view and change the way your BIOS accesses your hard disk, run your computer's CMOS Setup program. If you see an access mode such as CHS, Cylinder, Head, Sector, or Large Drive, try changing the setting to LBA. Save your change to the CMOS settings and try partitioning your hard disk again. If your problem goes away, you will know your BIOS supports the LBA required accessing your entire drive.

If your problem does not go away, you may be able to get updated BIOS from your COMPUTER vendor. If not, look for a driver that came with your hard drive or COMPUTER. Many vendors include OEM versions of Micro House Solutions EZ-Drive (**http://solutions.microhouse.com/products/ezdrive**) or on track Disk Manager Disk Go (**http://www.ontrack.com**). If so, install it.

14. Some of my files suddenly become corrupt, unreadable, or even vanish; Solution: bugs or user error, accidental deletions, renaming, and so on causes many file system mysteries. Nevertheless, if these

problems occur often, your file system may have become corrupted. On the other hand, you may have a virus.

First, have a good anti virus program. Keep it up to date by looking for vendor's web page for updates or patches. Last but not less run you're anti virus program often.

Many things can cause file system corruption-power failures; system hangs during a disk write; bugs in programs; intermittently defective RAM, hard disks or hard disk controllers; even Windows itself. A file's directory entry can be overwritten, causing it to vanish. Or the data the file contains may be unexpectedly altered, causing program crashes and data loss.

To fix these problems, and prevent their spread, run a file system integrity check program such as ScanDisk Start/Programs/Accessories/System Tools.

ScanDisk performs two types of checks. The Standard Test examines every directory entry on a disk, detecting and correcting corrupted or invalid file names, modification and creation dates, and file sizes. It also examines the disk's file allocation table, correcting errors such as disk regions neither allocated nor free, or both allocated and free. The Thorough Test reads every sector of a disk, both allocated and unallocated. If it can not read a sector because of a disk surface flaw, ScanDisk attempts to recover the information from the bad sector by reading it repeatedly. It then moves the information to a spare sector. You should run ScanDisk often-ideally once a week. Win98 and the Win95 Plus Pack include a program called System Agent, which lets you schedule tasks like ScanDisk to run at set intervals.

15. My favorite program keeps crashing; Solution: Sometimes, a crash is just a transient problem remedied by a reboot. However, if a problem persists for example, if you crash at the same point in a program or

process every time. On the other hand, if your program won't run at all, what then?

First, make sure that the program will work with your operation system version. e.g., not all Windows 98 programs will work with Windows Millennium Edition. So, read your programs requirements before you buy make sure it works with your operation system version.

Make sure the problem isn't the result of malfunctioning software by checking the vendor's Web site for patches or updates. Next, try a simple reinstall over the existing program. In most cases, this preserves any settings changes you made but will correct erroneous settings and replace corrupted DLLs.

If a simple reinstall does not work, try completely uninstalling the errant software, then rebooting and reinstalling from scratch. A clean start will often correct pernicious problems.

16. Every time I open Windows, it tries to dial out; Solution: Any number of things can cause this. First, make sure your Startup folder does not contain a shortcut to a program that automatically dials your ISP for you, if the program is configured to check for updates each time it's used. In case of doubt, remove faxing and other modem-related programs from the Startup group until you find the culprit, especially those with names like Windows Update, Live Update or similar.

If this does not help, open the Registry's HKEY_CURRENT_USER and HKEY_LOCAL_MACHINE keys one at a time. Drill down to the 1/4Software1/4Microsoft1/4Windows1/4CurrentVersion1/4Run sub key in both, and the1/4RunServices sub key in HKEY_LOCAL_MACHINE.

If you see an Internet-related program in the Name column, export the key, then delete that line. Keep an eye out for EXE files whose names you don't recognize; they may indicate a virus.

If this resolves the problem, you can probably reconfigure the program so that it stays away from the modem until you instruct it to make a connection. If so, make the configuration change and import the exported sub key to restore the former configuration.

It's possible a program listed on the run=line in WIN.INI is causing the problem, in which case the same general procedures should help to resolve it.

17. My network won't work; Solution: Often, Windows networking can mysteriously die, especially in upgrades where non-Microsoft networking clients, protocols and services previously were installed. Everything programmed to be installed and configured properly, but the Windows client just can not see the server or peers on the network. Networking problems can also cause subtle and hard-to-diagnose trouble with dial-up access.

A kind of networking housecleaning may fix things. First, make note of any networking settings so you can properly recreate them later, then use Control Panel's Network program to remove all clients, protocols, adapters, and services. If Dial-Up Networking is also a problem, delete all DUN connections after noting their settings.

Now reboot, reenter Control Panel, and reinstall all the necessary clients, protocol, adapters, and services in the Network program. Reboot again and rebuild your DUN connections.

This process-laborious but not difficult-refreshes all the elements of your networking plumbing and ensures all your drivers and clients are from the same release of Windows.

18. I can not log on to the network; Solution: With so many components in the chain-NICs, cables, hubs and OS drivers-troubleshooting network connections is never easy. You have to approach the problem systematically. First, check the obvious. Make sure all cables are securely connected to their ports in the NIC and hub, link/activity lights are on, and all equipment is compatible i.e., 10Mb per second NICs with 10Mbps hubs, 100Mbps NICs with 100Mbps hubs. A lot of equipment can operate at both 10Mbps and 100Mbps, so if the equipment does not auto sense the speed, make sure you manually set it on all devices in the connection. Some older auto sensing 10/100Mbps NICs choose a speed, and are locked into it until you power down and back up again. So if you manually switch hub speed from 10Mbps to 100Mbps and experience problems, turn off the machine with the NIC and turn it back on again.

The cable may be your problem, even if all link/activity lights are on. Ethernet wires are crimped into RJ-45 jacks and they can slip enough to break the connection. Test them with an Ohm/Power meter set to indicate when there's continuity between the pins on each side of the wire. This also helps you verify the wires are pinned straight through, not crossed.

If all is well on the physical side but problems, persist. Use WINI-COMPUTERFG.EXE AICOMPUTERONFIG.EXE in NT@ to ensure the OS knows the NIC is operational, and that the proper protocols IP/IPX. In addition, on are loaded and bound to the NIC. NICs that aren't loaded properly won't show up here. If everything checks out, use PING.EXE to test communications with other machines preferably local using TCP/IP, or with machines that are reliably up on the Internet, make sure you dial into your ISP first. For instance, "ping ftp.somewhere.com" will report a series of "reply" messages with response time in milliseconds. If you know the actual IP address (**www.xxx.yyy.zzz**) of the machine you are trying to reach, use that instead of the qualified domain name. This eliminates the possibility of a faulty DNS setting. If you don't know one, ping a server by name and the ping will give you the IP address. If pinging an IP address does not work, remove the NIC's network configuration entry and reboot. Windows should recognize the NIC and reinstall it for you. You may need to reinstall and reconfigure your TCP/IP protocol settings as well.

4

How to Diagnose Case Problems

The case is essentially a shell and not prone to causing operating problems. However, here are a few instances where the case may at the root of the problem.

It makes a squealing or other loud noise the power supply fan is failing and needs replacement. Usually the power supply is replaced, but some PC cases have the power supply permanently installed. Replace the case with one that has removable power supply.

Nothing happens when I turn on the PC Check that it is securely plugged into the outlet and into the back of the PC.

Check that the outlet has power.

Check for a second power switch near the power supply.

The main power switch has failed and needs to be replaced.

The power supply has failed and needs to be replaced.

I hear a rattling sound Make sure that the case shell or cover is properly installed and secured. The PC randomly shuts itself off The power supply could be overheating, check that the fan is working.

Check any secondary cooling fans for proper operation.

The power supply could be failing.

Clean out all dust and clear the air intakes.

Make sure that the case shell or cover is properly installed and secured.

Use caution:

Before opening the case, unplug the PC to avoid an electrical shock hazard. Exercise caution, as there are sharp edges on a PC and its components. Always wear a static electricity discharge strap when working with your PC's components to avoid damaging your PC. Note that some manufacturers will void your PC's warranty if you open the case.

Replacing your computer's case can be a major undertaking. Although it requires no complicated installations or reconfiguration, nearly every component must be removed and reinstalled in the new case.

When removing the components of the PC, be sure to place them on a clean, dry surface. Do not place them on carpeting or other static prone material. Handle all components by their edges and avoid touching the electronics.

Unplug the PC.

Static electricity is harmless to you but it can fry your computer chips. Static electricity is mainly caused by dry air and or friction e.g., dragging your feet across a carpet. It's best to use a grounding strip. Or touch the metal frame of your case to complete the ground before you unplug it. This does not work as well but it is better to be safe then sorry. To lower the risk of static electricity, avoid standing on carpet. Ideally, you should have your computer set up on a grounding mat. Consult your manual if you need help opening your computer's case.

Unplug the power supply connector from the motherboard and each of the components. Disconnect the lead to the on/off switch (or remove the entire switch). Disconnect the case control wires, such as the PC speaker, hard drive activity LED etc. from the motherboard.

Disconnect the floppy drive, hard drive and CD-ROM ribbon connectors from the motherboard. To avoid confusion during reassemble, label the connector that was connected to the primary IDE controller. The primary IDE controller should be labeled on the motherboard and "PRI IDE", "IDE 1" or something similar.

Remove the screws that secure each of the accessory cards to the case. If the motherboard has no obstructions blocking it, it may be possible to leave all of the cards in their slots and remove the entire motherboard intact. If so, skip to step. Otherwise, make a written note of which card is installed in which slot and remove the cards.

Remove the screws that secure the motherboard to the case. Instead of screws the motherboard may use plastic snaps. To release the snaps, pinch the plastic tip together while gently lifting the motherboard.

Remove each of the drives, noting which cable is connected. If more than one device is connected to a cable, note the order of the drives.

Inspect the new case and determine the best order for installing the components. In some situations, the drives may interfere with the installation of the motherboard or vice versa. Go to step 14 first if you installing the drives before the motherboard?

Install the plastic or metal mounting posts into the case so they will align with the holes in the motherboard. Secure the board in place by snapping it in over the plastic posts or fastening it with screws.

Connect the power supply to the motherboard. Insert the drives into the appropriate bays. Make certain that the controller cables and electrical wires can reach each of the drives. Fasten each drive in place with the original screws.

Connect the case control wires to the motherboard. Most cases will have a wire for the PC speaker, reset switch, hard disk activity LED, and power LED. Some cases will have wire for the power switch. If there is a wire for "Turbo" it usually serves no purpose and can be ignored.

Install the drive controller ribbon cables to their appropriate drive controllers on the motherboard. Make certain that you align pin #1 of the cables with pin #1 of the controller.

Connect the power supply to each of the drives.

If they were removed, reinstall each of the accessory cards.

If it was connected before, reconnect the CD-ROM sound output to the sound card.

Double-check each of your steps.

Reconnect the keyboard, mouse and monitor.

Plugs in the power supply and test the PC.

If the system boots properly, shut it down and replace the case. Also reconnect any other wires to the back of the PC.

If there are any problems, the most likely cause is a loose, unconnected or improperly connected card or wire. Shut down and unplug the PC and check all of the connections.

5

Diagnosing PC Hardware Problems

When I turn it on…It makes no sound and there are no lights

Check the Power Supply

Check the Motherboard

Check the CPU

When I turn it on…It just beeps

Read our Beep Codes List

Check the Keyboard

Check the Video Card

Check the Memory

Check the Motherboard

When I turn it on…It sounds normal but the screen is blank

Check the Video Card

When I turn it on…It starts up but never loads the operating system

Check the Hard Disk

Check the Memory

Check the Motherboard

Check the CPU

When I turn it on…It freezes BEFORE the operating system starts loading

Check the Keyboard

Check the Video Card

Check the Memory

Check the RLINK"../hardware/power/power.htm"Power Supply

Check the Motherboard

Check the CPU

When I turn it on…

It freezes WHILE the operating system is loading

This is probably a software problem not covered in this hardware guide. If you are using Windows, try booting into safe mode by holding down the "F8" key or in some cases the "CONTROL" key.

While it is on…It makes a screeching or other loud noise

Check the Power Supply Fan

Check the CPU Fan

Check any other Internal Fans

Check the CD-ROM

Check the Hard Disk

Check the Floppy Drive

While it is on…It shuts itself off

Check the power features in the BIOS

Check the power features in the Windows Control Panel

Check the Power Supply

If the problem occurs in association with a specific hardware component, visit the diagnostic page for that particular part. Software Issues are not covered in this hardware guide.

6

ScanDisk and Defragmenter

You should always-run ScanDisk before you run the Defragmenter. Scandisk looks for and fixes any errors on you hard drive. Use this system utility to make your PC more stable and run faster.

Prepare to ScanDisk

Go to your start if you're using Windows 98, go to the Start menu, and select Programs, Accessories, System Tools, and finally ScanDisk. After you start the program, you should be should that you have the following box 1. "Standard" this checks files and folders for errors. And 2. Automatically fix errors, it does just what it says. You only need to run Thorough If you install a new hard drive in. Alternatively, if you think you may be having hard drive problems. It performs Standard test and scans the disk surface for errors.

As you use your computer, files are spread out all over your hard-disk drive. That slows it down because it takes longer to find the data it needs. When you defragment, you optimize your disk, which puts all the files in one place and speeds up disk access.

Prepare to Defragment

Start by preparing your hard drive for optimization. You should uninstall any unneeded programs, remove any data files you no longer want, empty the recycle bin, and most importantly back up your data. Defragmentation is generally a safe process, but it's not worth taking any chances.

Now you're ready to defragment. If you're using Windows 98, go to the Start menu and select Programs, Accessories, System Tools, and finally Disk Defragmenter. This would be a good time for a break. It takes a while to defragment a hard drive, especially if you've never done it before.

After you're through, all your files will be optimized and in one place. You should notice an improvement in the speed of your computer right away.

See you can do it yourself!

You should run ScanDisk any time you get error messages. A most of time ScanDisk can find the problems and fix them. You should run defrag after you install or uninstall any program.

7

How To: Install a Printer

If you've recently purchased a printer or plan to buy one soon, you're going to need an idea of what to do after you take it out of the box. Configuring a printer should be a hassle-free process thanks to a feature in Windows called Plug-n-Play.

Plug-n-Play automatically senses when you've connected a printer to the parallel or USB ports on your computer and immediately tries to load the correct printer drivers.

Plug-n-Play also initiates when you've inserted anything into a PCI or AGP slot or connected a PS/2 or serial cable to your PC. It's a neat feature, but do you know how to install a printer if it doesn't work correctly?

Gather all the components that came with your printer—manuals, printer cartridges, cables, power adapter, disks, and paper—and continue reading if you'd like to learn how to configure and install a printer. You may also need a copy of your operating system, so have that disk handy just in case.

Plug-n-Play Printer Install

Use these general steps to configure a printer before it's installed. When in doubt, reference the manual that came with your printer.

Start by unpacking the printer from its box (if it isn't already). Connect the power supply to the printer and don't forget to plug it into a power source.

Insert any ink cartridges inside your printer. Don't forget to pull the protective tab off the ink cartridge.

Load a stack of paper into the paper tray and make sure to shut the tray all the way when you've finished.

Chances are that when you bought a printer you had a good idea of how it was going to connect to your PC. All consumer-level printers connect to your PC via either its parallel or USB ports. Here's a graphic displaying the difference between the two.

Locate the correct cable, either parallel or USB, and connect it to your printer.

The final step is to connect the other end of that cable to your PC's parallel or USB ports. At this time you should notice Plug-n-Play trying to install the correct printer drivers.

Let the wizard walk you through installing the drivers.

Try printing a test page after the drivers are installed.

If Plug-n-Play doesn't prompt you to install anything after you've connected the printer cable to your PC, then this feature may be disabled in your BIOS. That's OK. There's another way to install the correct drivers.

Manual Printer Install

If Plug-n-Play isn't successful, you do have another option for installing a printer.

Single-click the Start menu, mouse over Settings, and then single-click Printers.

When the printers dialog box appears, double-click the Add Printer icon to launch the wizard.

Click the Next button on the wizard.

Choose Local Printer and then select the Next button.

Wait for the wizard to build a driver database list.

Select the manufacturer of your printer from the list.

Select the correct printer model. Click the Next button on the wizard.

Choose the correct printer port. By default it should be LPT1. The default setting is the one you want. Click the Next button on the wizard. Fill in a name for your new printer. If you'd like the printer to be your default printer mark the Yes box. Click the Next button on the wizard.

If you'd like to print a test page, leave the next field alone and press the Next button.

At this time you'll be prompted to insert your Windows disk before going any further. Do this now.

Press OK to complete the driver installation.

If everything goes OK, you should have a nice test page printed on your new printer. Continue reading, because there's one last step to take before your new printer is fully ready to go.

Install Printer Disk

The last step is to load the disk that came with your printer into your CD-ROM. This disk should contain the latest drivers for your printer along with additional programs and shareware. You can browse this disk at your leisure.

If your printer is working, you may not need to do anything else. But you should consider updating your printer driver with the one that's on the disk to increase printer performance. Usually, the disk that comes with a new printer should have a more recent version of the printer driver than the one that shipped with Windows.

8

Removing and replacing the battery

Unplug the PC

Static electricity is harmless to you but it can fry your computer chips. It's best to use a grounding strip or touch the metal frame of your case to complete the ground. This does not work as well but it is better to be safe then sorry.

Introduction

This document describes how to remove and replace the CMOS battery in PCs. The Setup information is stored in CMOS RAM and is backed up by a battery when power to the system is off. The battery also keeps the system clock current. As long as the internal battery remains good and is connected, the clock continues to keep the date and time accurately and the Setup information will remain intact.

WARNING: There is danger of explosion if the battery is not correctly replaced.

To remove and replace the CMOS battery, go through the following instructions.

Before removing the battery, you must first remove the system cover and get access to the motherboard. Follow the procedure below to remove the system cover.

Observe all Safety and ESD precautions stated above.

Turn off all peripherals connected to the system.

Identify and tag all cables. Disconnect the cables from the system.

Remove the two screws that secure the back panel to the chassis.

Once the screws have been removed, pull back and up on the back panel and the two clips on the bottom of the panel will naturally disengage.

The left side panel is the panel on the left of the system when facing the front of the system. Support the front edge of the left side panel with one hand while grasping the rear of the panel.

Pull towards the back of the system until the panel separates from the front of the chassis.

Pull the now loose panel away from the system.

Gaining access to the battery

To remove the battery, you need access to the part of the motherboard that holds the battery. Computers have different motherboards, which have different battery locations. On some computers, you can remove and replace the battery without removing any of the I/O cards (such as the modem and sound adapter cards). On other computers, you have to remove all I/O cards.

Removing and replacing the battery

The battery simply slides out of the battery housing. Slide it out and replace it with the same manufacturer's Lithium battery type. Discard the used battery according to the manufacturer's instructions.

9

What is cache memory?

It's the area of memory that stores the most-recently-accessed data. When a computer needs data once, chances are it will need it again, soon; so computer designers realized they could speed up the computer by storing the most recently accessed data in a high-speed storage area.

Most caches are FIFO (first in, first out). This means that, as the cache fills, the older data is thrown out. This makes sense because you want the most-recently-accessed data available. So as data ages, it falls out of the cache to make room for the newer data.

There are several types of cache on your computer: Disk cache. Current Windows versions have this, though you can't see it or set it. It reserves an area of RAM to store data that has been accessed from the hard drive. So if the data is requested again from the hard drive, the computer gets it from RAM, which is much faster.

Hardware cache. Many hard drives have cache. Almost all CD drives have cache; most have 256K or 512K. It speeds up access to the CD and the CD's performance.

Browser cache. This saves data from recently accessed websites on the hard drive and pulls it off the hard drive if you ask for that information again, instead of taking the time to get it from the Internet. This can really speed up your browsing. Netscape calls it "cache," while Internet Explorer calls it "temporary Internet files."

Application cache. This type of cache is similar to the others, except it's application specific. For example, Microsoft Word has its own type of cache, but it works much like the others.

Processor Cache. There are several types:

Level 1 (L1). Located inside the processor itself, L1 is very fast because the processor doesn't have to go far to get that data. It's usually a small amount because processor real estate is expensive. Intel's first Celeron processor has no cache, but the company gave the Celeron A 128K of internal cache. The Pentium II separates the cache from the main chip but keeps it on the board. This is a disadvantage because the PII cache runs at one-half the processor speed. This is why the Celeron A processor can be faster than a PII, even with less cache.

The new AMD K62 has 64K L1 cache.

Level 2 (L2). L2 cache is usually on the motherboard. Most boards come with 512K L2 cache. Some have a full megabyte. There are faster types of L2 cache that use pipeline burst cache.

10

All about RAM and How to Add RAM

To see the best results from a RAM upgrade you'll most likely want to slot RAM sticks according to size. If your older RAM is of smaller size, you'll want to reconfigure the order. Consult your manual for help if you don't know your motherboard's slot order.

When you purchase new memory you need to get RAM that is compatible with your motherboard. There are various ways to figure this out. One way is to go directly to your motherboard manufacturer's website and look up your motherboard model's specifications.

Another idea is to try a major memory vendor and see if it provides a tool for identifying compatibility between motherboards and memory sticks. There are many out there. I like Kingston's Memory Configuration. Try it out before you purchase new memory.

Before you purchase anything, take a look and see what the specs are on your old RAM. You'll understand why you need to do this after reading this article. Check carefully to make sure you're not mixing and matching different types of RAM.

As faster and more capable computers evolve, so does the RAM that acts to enhance their capabilities. You will see terms such as SDRAM, SLDRAM, EDRAM, VRAM, and EPROM all thrown about by techies and non-techies alike. Most of these many acronyms are either names for faster memory types and prototypes or specific to hardware such as Video RAM (VRAM). Manufacturers put the best kind of memory available to them on computers, printers, and so on. If you choose to upgrade or add RAM, you will need to find out what kind of RAM you already have and what is compatible with your hardware. Static RAM doesn't lose its contents but holds them from point to point. This type is not very common in personal computers. It's more commonly found in handheld devices.

Electronically Programmable RAM holds its contents almost forever, but can be programmed by software. EEPROM is electrically erasable and programmable, and shining a light into the top of the RAM erases PROM. RAM is your PC's workspace. Your CPU takes data off a drive, typically the hard drive, and temporarily stores it in RAM. RAM stands for Random Access Memory because it can be accessed randomly. In other words, any byte of memory can be accessed without touching the preceding bytes. Dynamic RAM (DRAM) is the most common type of RAM. It accesses information, as it needs it, then closes and goes on to something else. Because it's random, pieces of information can be stacked one upon another, without discarding the entire stack. Picture a deck of cards, where cards can be added to the top, bottom, or inserted in the middle. Cards can also be withdrawn from any of these areas as well, either to be removed from the deck, or just shuffled to another part.

The information in DRAM is not only Dynamic and Randomly accessed, it is also fast. Today's processors handle information so fast that they require a steady flow of information to optimize their capabilities. While hard drives offer plenty of storage space at a low cost per megabyte, their rotating parts and small buffering systems are too slow to keep up with the processor's need for input. Because DRAM is solid state (with no moving parts), it can send data as fast as the processor can keep up with it. RAM is fast but also volatile. It has no way of holding onto the data it stores. We pull information from our slow-but-stable hard drives into memory, which then handles it at speeds fast enough for the processor to work with it. The amount of RAM you have definitely impacts your performance. Consider the analogy of a basic workspace, such as a drawing board. More memory lets you create a larger drawing table to work on. This means that you can lay out more of your project at one time, and work on it all at once. In addition, you can have more tools, such as markers, brushes, straight edges, and pencils at your elbow. If your table is smaller, you may have to go over to the counter when you need a specific tool, or file some pages away before you get any more. This process of putting away and getting out is very slow. If your space is extremely small, you may find that tools and artwork are just too close together and that your space is cluttered. When this happens, you slow things down even more, and run the risk of spilling, tearing, or smudging the work. RAM is your PC's workspace. Your CPU takes data off a drive, typically the hard drive, and temporarily stores it in RAM (Random Access Memory). Mixing RAM can be tricky. Always check your motherboard manual or your computer manual before adding RAM. In general, the combination you propose will work, although not all combinations of RAM work. SDRAM is short for Synchronous Dynamic RAM. SDRAM synchronizes itself with your CPU's motherboard speed—BUS speed. If your computer has 66-MHz BUS, it is possible to buy a higher-speed RAM. The 100 Hz will slow down and work just fine. You can buy 100-Hz RAM and put it in a slower motherboard, but you will have problems if you try to migrate 66 MHz into a faster 100-MHz motherboard. This is called over clocking, which is running a chip at a speed higher than it's rated for. This can be risky, as there are potential side effects with over clocking, such as overheating the chip.

DIMMS vs. SIMMs

Check your computer manual for the kind of memory you need. There are two main kinds of memory: DIMMs are longer and have two notches along the bottom, while SIMMs are a little shorter and have a single notch. There are different kinds of DIMMs and SIMMs as well. Your manual will tell you which kind you need.

Open your computer. Your manual will come in handy here, too, because every computer case is different. Once you've got the computer open, it's time to ground yourself—self to drain off any static for charge. ***Static Electricity is harmless to you but it can fry your computer chips. It's best to use a grounding strip. You can find one at almost any electronic store for just a few dollars. If you can't find one, make sure to touch a metal part of your computer's case to discharge any static.***

It's time to add the memory. SIMM slots are white and held in place by clips at each end. Insert the SIMM at a 45-degree angle and gently tilt it up until it's upright. The clips should snap into place and the SIMM should be firmly held in its slot. If it's wobbly or uneven, release the clips and try again.

Adding DIMM

DIMM slots are black and held by larger tabs. Insert the DIMM upright. Release the tabs then gently push the DIMM into place. The tabs should snap up, lock, and hold the memory into place.

Once you've added memory, turn on your PC. It should recognize the new memory automatically. Again, check your manual for any exceptions to this rule.

You should now realize a performance increase. Generally, Windows 95 machines should have at least 32MB of memory, Macintosh users should also use about 32MB, and if you're using Windows NT, 48MB seems to be the minimum.

DIMMs vs. SIMMs

Now open up your computer. Your manual will come in handy here, too, because every computer case is different.

Once you've got the computer open, it's time to ground yourself—that's to drain off any static charge. Static electricity is harmless to you but it can fry your computer chips. It's best to use a grounding strip; you can find one at almost any electronic store for just a few dollars. If you can't find one, make sure to touch a metal part of your computer's case to discharge any static

Add SIMMs

Now it's time to add the memory. SIMM slots are white and are held in place by clips at each end. Insert the SIMM at a 45-degree angle and gently tilt it up until it's upright. The clips should snap into place and the SIMM should be firmly held in its slot. If it's wobbly or uneven, release the clips and try again.

Add DIMMs

DIMM slots are black and are held by larger tabs. Insert the DIMM upright. Release the tabs then gently push the DIMM into place. The tabs should snap up, lock, and hold the memory into place.

Memory Needs

Once you've added your memory, turn on your PC. It should recognize the new memory automatically. Again, check your manual for any exceptions to this rule.

That's it! You've added more memory to your computer and you should realize a real performance increase.

11

How to Install a Internal Modem

The modem is a device that enables the PC to use a telephone line to communicate with other PCs, devices and the Internet. The modem plugs into a slot on the motherboard. It converts data into signals that can be transmitted over the telephone line and receives data that is converted back for the PC to use

How to Install a Internal Modem

Unplug the PC

Static electricity is harmless to you but it can fry your computer chips. Static electricity is mainly caused by dry air and or friction e.g., dragging your feet across a carpet. It's best to use a grounding strip. Or touch the metal frame of your case to complete the ground before you unplug it. This does not work as well but it is better to be safe then sorry. To lower the risk of static electricity, avoid standing on carpet. Ideally, you should have your computer set up on a grounding mat. Consult your manual if you need help opening your computer's case.

Always wear a static electricity discharge strap when working with your PC's components to avoid damaging your PC. Always follow the manufacturer's instructions that were supplied with your modem.

An internal modem is easy to install. Most PCs use a PCI slot for a modem. Older PCs used an ISA slot; which is now obsolete. Check that you have an available slot and the slot type, before purchasing a modem.

Remove the cover plate adjacent to the slot for your modem.

Align the modem over the slot with the phone jack facing toward the outside of the PC Set the modem into the slot and press down firmly. Make sure the mounting bracket is properly aligned with any slot that might be present. It may be necessary to gently rock the modem from end to end to secure it in the slot. The gold contacts at the bottom of the modem should nearly or completely disappear into the slot. The card should be level and straight. Secure the modem-mounting bracket to the case with a screw (or replace the securing mechanism your case uses.

Replace the cover.Plug all of the PC cables back in. You know the mouse, keyboard, speakers and what every else you have. Plug in the telephone wire to the modem jack labeled ALine@ and plugs the other end into the telephone outlet on the wall. You may also plug a telephone into the modem jack labeled "Phone". Then plug the power back in. Always plug power in last. That completes the hardware installation, next you will need to start the computer and complete the software installation. Your modem should have come with a disk that contains the appropriate drivers for your modem. Follow the manufacturer's instructions for installing the software. Windows will detect the modem and start the hardware wizard; simply follow the prompts. Some manufacturers require you to cancel the hardware wizard and complete the installation using manufacturer installation instructions. This works best for me.

12

How to connect an external modem

To connect an external modem to your computer, you'll need a serial modem cable. Most likely, your computer will have a connector on the back labeled serial, or with the IOIOIO icon. This connector comes in two varieties: 9-pin (male) or 25-pin (female). If you only have one of these ports, it will probably be COM1. If you have two, one will be COM1, and the other will be COM2. After you plug in your modem, you can sign up for Internet service.

Usually your setup program will try and find your modem and its COM port. If it can't, it will ask you which COM port your modem is attached to. If you don't know, the easiest thing to do is try them all. Even if you only have two serial ports, you may be able to select one of four COM ports. Also, there are some other devices that use the COM ports. In some computers the mouse is plugged into a serial port. This is known as a serial mouse. If you've got a serial mouse plugged into COM1, then just plug the modem into COM2. If you don't have a second COM port, you can purchase a card that goes inside your computer that will give you a second COM port. If this is necessary, you should check with the manufacturer of your computer.

Your modem will likely have a connector on the back with space for 25 pins. You need to make sure that the serial modem cable you purchase has the right number of pins on either side and is the correct "gender." The best thing to do is to look at the back of your computer and list the various connectors, the number of pins, and the gender. When you go to purchase your modem, find the cable that matches the connector.

Lastly, you'll need a standard phone cable to connect the modem to your phone line. The standard connector on a telephone cable is called an RJ-11. On the back of your modem, you'll probably have two RJ-11 jacks. One is for connecting the modem to a wall jack, and the other is for connecting the modem to a telephone.

13

The Floppy Drive and What is does

The floppy disk drive is a device that records data onto a removable storage disk called a floppy disk. Floppy disks, also called "floppies", are the most basic storage medium for data. However their limited capacity, typically 1.44 megabytes, makes them of limited use.

A floppy disk can be used to copy files from one PC to another PC or for making backup copies of files.

Replacing a floppy drive is very easy and inexpensive to do should the need arise.

PC based floppies only a hand few of years ago were 5.25 inches. Before the mainstream introduction of the home computer, floppies of 8 and 10 inches were in wide use. Now floppies have a more rigid outer shell and are 3.5 inches. However their low capacity make them of limited value.

Floppy capacities, in the PC era, started at 360KB, climbed to 1.2MB then the smaller 3.5 inch floppy was introduced. The new floppy could hold 720KB of data and then doubled to 1.44MB in 1987. A 2.88MB disk was developed by Toshiba but it never caught on.

There are a couple of other removable media disk products on the market, such as the Iomega ZIP drive. These specialized drives use a proprietary disk media to record considerably more data than will fit on a conventional floppy.

How to Diagnose Floppy Drive Problems

These are some symptoms that may be caused by the floppy drive. Other components may also cause these same symptoms, check the general diagnosis page for more information.

Indicator light never goes on Check that the power connector is properly and securely connected.

Check that the interface cable to properly and securely connected to both the drive and the motherboard.

Indicator light never goes off the interface cable may be reversed. Check the connection to the drive and to the motherboard.

Drive type mismatch during boot Check for proper configuration in CMOS.

The floppy drive may need to be replaced.

"Invalid media" or "Track 00 bad" error when formatting the floppy disk may be defective.

The drive may not be properly configured in CMOS.

You may be using the wrong floppy disk density for your drive.

The same directory is displayed for different diskettes refresh the view.

Reinsert the disk, making sure it goes in all the way.

Check that the interface cable to properly and securely connected to both the drive and the motherboard. The floppy drive may need to be replaced.

"Drive not ready" error there is no disk in the floppy drive.

Reinsert the disk, making sure it goes in all the way.

The floppy drive may need to be replaced.

"General failure" error the disk in the drive is not formatted.

You may be using the wrong floppy disk density for your drive.

The drive is out of alignment.. "Sector not found" error the drive is out of alignment.

How to Replace a Floppy Drive

Unplug the PC

Static electricity is harmless to you but it can fry your computer chips.It's best to use a grounding strip or touch the metal frame of your case to complete the ground. This does not work as well but it is better to be safe then sorry

Disconnect all wires from the back of the PC.

Open the case.

If replacing a floppy drive disconnect the power and interface cables from the drive and remove the retaining screws from either side of the drive.

Identify the position of the #1 pin on the interface connection on the back of the drive.

Choose the location for the floppy drive so that the drive will have a opening in the case's face plate and so that the power and interface cables will reach the drive.

Mount the drive so that he eject button is under (not over) the slot for the floppy.

Connect the interface cable so that the cable's #1 pin matches the drives #1 pin.

Connect the power wire to the drive.

Position the drive and secure with the mounting screws. Always use the screws supplied by the manufacturer. Screws of the wrong size or length can damage the drive.

If it is not already, connect the interface cable to the motherboard's controller labeled "FDD" so that the cable's #1 pin matches the motherboard's #1 pin.

Double check all of your connections.

Replace the cover.

Reconnect the wires removed in step 2.

Plug in the PC.

It may be necessary to configure this drive in the CMOS.

14

Video cards 101

Buying a high performance graphics card may seem like it requires an advanced engineering degree. The terminology is obscure, performance ratings conflict, and upgrades come even faster than they do for CPUs. But you can make an informed choice. And no matter what you choose, even the poorest cards today outperform the best cards of a year ago for a fraction of the cost.

How a Video Card Works

How do the instructions written in a piece of software end up as a recognizable image on your computer screen? The essential piece of hardware in this process is the video card, but other players are in the drama. Remember that we're covering video cards in general, not 3D graphics accelerators.

Let's use a bit-map file to explain how information written in software is sent through a graphics adapter and ultimately displayed on a computer screen. A bit-map file is a representation of a graphical image, consisting of rows and columns and dots. The bit-map file determines the width, height, and color of a given image. In the case of 24-bit graphics, for example, three bytes of memory are used to define each of the many pixels that make up the pictures that appear on your computer screen. Each of the three bytes determines how much red, green, and blue are in each pixel. Using these three colors, virtually any other color can be displayed (16 million total).

The software containing the bit-map file sends it to the computer's graphics adapter. Within the graphics adapter are units of RAM called frame buffers. The frame buffers store a value for each of the pixels that compose the display image on your computer screen. The adapter takes the information stored in the frame buffer and adjusts the intensity of the red, blue, and green values that make up each pixel.

From the frame buffers the information is sent to a chip that also lies on the graphics adapter. It's called a digital-to-analog converter, or DAC. The DAC takes the digital value that's stored in the frame buffers and converts it to analog form so that it can be displayed on the computer screen.

The computer monitor continuously receives electrical instructions from the DAC. As the information is received, the monitor fires its electron guns at the colored phosphors that are painted onto the inside of the computer screen according to how intense a particular color should be relative to the other two in a given pixel.

In the last few years, video cards have seen tremendous gains in both performance and display quality. With winter in full swing, video card manufacturers are delivering their latest and fastest hardware to those folks willing to pay a premium.

Read on to see if you really need that pricey new card. Then see how some of the new video screamers reacted to our tests. Today's video cards depend on a variety of system resources—especially the CPU. In addition to feeding the video card with the information it needs to function smoothly, the CPU must also perform the bidding of any active resident programs. Those programs include what is usually the biggest resident of all: the operating system. Modern video cards can churn through more data than all but the fastest CPUs can provide. Any load you can remove from the CPU will translate into increased video performance. But this will only get you so far.

Buying a new video card with an aging CPU is a recipe for sluggishness. The cost of a top-of-the-line 3D video card is currently $200 to $300, depending on additional options. The cost for the fastest AMD CPU is less than half of that and less than all but the fastest Intel CPUs.

So before you plunk down your hard-earned cash on a new video card, consider upgrading your CPU. Last year, I upgraded a system from a 450 MHz processor to a speedy 800 MHz CPU (an inexpensive upgrade, if your current motherboard can support it) while continuing to use the same video hardware. Our gains in video performance with this single upgrade measured 50 to 100 percent, depending on the application. (The applications I used were none other than our favorite games.) 3D games are among the best real-world video-card benchmarks, due to their intense CPU usage and the demands they place on the video system.

If a slow CPU is already working overtime to perform the calculations required for a game, a high-end video card will spend more time sitting idle, waiting for new information. Therefore, if you don't run many programs (games) that require strong video hardware, consider saving that cash for future updates or a completely new system.

15

Install a Sound Card

Most new computers come with a sound card or audio capabilities built into the motherboard. While onboard audio is adequate for business use (word processing, spreadsheets, graphics), you will probably want to upgrade to a new sound card if you play games, create your own music, or edit video—any task where the sound is the primary experience or enhances it. Fortunately, installing a sound card is easy to do.

Disable onboard audio

Even if your computer's motherboard already has an onboard audio support, you can still install an upgraded sound card that will take precedence over the proprietary board.

Almost all onboard audio is controlled through the BIOS. To disable it, all you have to do is go into your computer's BIOS menus and find an option to disable the audio. The BIOS can be entered at the boot sequence by typing some variation of keys after the RAM test, usually Delete or F2. There is often even a message (although it flashes by quickly) informing you what to do to enter the BIOS.

Now that you are in the BIOS, there are several tabs or menu headings. One of the advanced menus will likely have the option for audio control. Be sure and remember exactly what you have changed, in case you want to go back later and change things back. After making any change in the BIOS, you will be prompted to save changes upon exit. Save your changes, shut down the computer, and unplug it.

Install the sound card

Now it's time to install the card.

Open the computer and find a free PCI slot (or ISA if you have an ISA sound card).

Carefully insert your sound card into the slot (using a little bit of pressure).

Secure the card by screwing it into the case.

Now you are ready to plug the power cord back in and turn the computer on.

If you are running Windows, there is a great chance it will detect that you have new hardware. Windows will look for drivers and you will likely be given the option "Have Disk." Insert the disk or CD that came with your sound card and select "Have Disk."

Windows should be able to locate the proper drivers to make your new sound card function. Don't expect any audible results until you've plugged your speakers into the new sound card.

If your operating system does not detect the new sound card, the software that came with the card should have some sort of installation procedure. Put the software in the appropriate drive and search for a "setup" or "install" file. Run that file and follow the instructions on the screen.

The last thing you can try (if running Windows) is to go into the control panel and select "Add/Remove" hardware. Scroll down to multimedia and let the computer attempt to detect the sound card. If

Windows fails at these efforts, you can still select the "Have Disk" option and follow the steps outlined above from that point.

16

CD-ROM and how to install

A CD-RW drive is a device that reads information or music off of a compact disk (CD) and can also write information to a CD. CD-RW stands for Compact Disc Read Write.

CD-RW can write only to disks that are designated for writing; either CD-R or CD-RW. Disks that are already recorded upon, such as music CDs and commercial software, cannot be accidentally recorded over. A CD-R can be recorded upon once and read forever. CD-RW can be recorded upon numerous times and read forever.

The CD is spun at high speed inside the drive while a laser is directed at the surface to read the data or music. The CD-ROM is referenced as a 12X or 12 speed (or any other number). This simply means that it spins the CD that many times faster than the original industry specification. So, a 48X CD-ROM spins the CD up to 48 times faster than the original specification. Faster is better.

A CD-RW's speed is referenced as 4X 2X 20X. The first number is the top speed for writing a CD. The second number is the top speed for rewriting a CD and the last number is the top speed for reading a CD.

Some older CD-ROMs and music CD players cannot read CD-Rs. However, most equipment manufactured since 1999 can read disks created on a PC.

For greatest operating efficiency, the CD-RW drive should be connected to the IDE controller that is not controlling the hard disk from which writing will usually be done. Although it can be connected to the IDE controller with the hard disk, only one device can communicate with the controller at a time thus causes a bottleneck. If you will be copying files from a hard disk that is on controller one, then put the CD-RW on controller two or vice versa.

Mini CD's and business card CD's are not recommended for use in a CD-ROM or CD-RW because of the risk of damage. Although mini CD's are convenient, they tend to become unstable and damage the drive.

How to Diagnose CD-RW Problems

I cannot access the drive and the light does not go on Check that the power and controller cables are securely attached to the drive.

Verify that pin #1 of the controller cable is matched to pin #1 on the drive and on the motherboard. The operating system may not be configured to use or "see" the drive. If it never worked, verify that the jumpers on the drive are set correctly.

I cannot access the drive but the light does go on The CD may be damaged or unreadable. Try removing and reinserting the disk.

Try cleaning the CD. Verify that pin #1 of the controller cable is matched to pin #1 on the drive and on the motherboard.

If it never worked, verify that the jumpers on the drive are set correctly.

The drive drawer will not open Press the button once and wait at least a minute. In Windows, go to "My Computer", right click on the CD-ROM drive and choose "Eject" from the menu. With the computer unplugged, you can open most CD-ROM drawers with a unwound paper clip. Poke it, as straight as possible, into the hole and push with moderate force (the paper clip may bend a little) to force the drawer opens a half-inch. Now pull the drawer the rest of the way open.

If the problem persists, check that the power connector and controller cable is securely connected to the drive. A CD may be jammed or broken inside the drive. Access may require the removal of the drive's outer case. If this is necessary, it is very likely that the drive will have to be replaced.

I hear it spinning and then stopping repeatedly The CD may be damaged or unreadable. Try removing and reinserting the disk.

Try cleaning the CD. Verify that pin #1 of the controller cable is matched to pin #1 on the drive and on the motherboard.

If it never worked, verify that the jumpers on the drive are set correctly.

The drive seems to transfer data too slowly Is the drive on the same controller cable as the primary hard drive? If so, performance will be slowed because only one device can communicate at a time. Move it to the second IDE controller.

Other problems, such as failure to write unreadable disks and slow operation are generally related to software issues and not covered here.

How to install a CD-ROM or CD-RW How to install a CD-ROM or CD-RW

Always follow the manufacturer's instructions:

Unplug the PC

Static electricity is harmless to you but it can fry your computer chips Static electricity is mainly caused by dry air and or friction e.g., dragging your feet across a carpet. It's best to use a grounding strip. Or touch the metal frame of your case to complete the ground before you unplug it. This does not work as well but it is better to be safe then sorry. To lower the risk of static electricity, avoid standing on carpet. Ideally, you should have your computer set up on a

grounding mat. Consult your manual if you need help opening your computer's case.

Open the case

If you are replacing a CD-ROM or CD-RW, disconnect the controller cable, power connector and audio connection (if present). Remove the retaining screws and remove the drive. Set the jumper to "Master" or "MA" if the drive will be the first or only drive on a controller. Set the jumper to "Slave" or "SL" if it will be the second drive on a controller. Insert the new drive into the bay used for the old drive, or select a bay that has a suitable corresponding opening in the case front. Make sure it is right side up (the button should be under the drawer). Secure the drive in place with the provided screws or rail inserts.

Connect the controller cable to the drive and the motherboard (the controller that is not controlling the hard disk that you will usually be writing from is strongly recommended). Make sure that pin #1 of the cable corresponds to pin #1 on the drive and motherboard. If you have two connectors to choose from, use the one at the end. Connect the power to the drive. Connect the audio wire (if one is being used) to the drive and to the sound card or motherboard. Close the case.

Then plug the power back in. Always plug power in last. The device will have to be configured for use by your operating system and software drivers installed. Also, CD burner software will be has to be installed before you can start writing to CD-Rs.

When installing any type of new CD drive on your computer, several items should be taken into consideration. Let's take a look at installing a drive to the IDE chain inside your PC.

IDE

Most motherboards have primary and secondary IDE channels that are capable of supporting up to four IDE devices. Generally, the hard drive and an existing CD-ROM drive use one of these channels. If you have more than one hard drives, more than one CD drive (ROM, DVD, or RW), or a Zip or tape drive, you want to make sure that you still have space for the new CD drive. In other words, make sure you haven't exceeded the four device capacity, including the new drive you want to install.

Once you have verified that you have room for the new drive, you will need to determine which devices are "master" devices and which are "slaves." You can find this by following these steps:

When you boot up your computer, it will automatically detect your IDE devices. It will tell you whether the device is a primary or secondary master/slave.

You can also enter into the CMOS on boot up and it should list your devices (sometimes, depending on who makes your motherboard) and specify which are primary or secondary master/slave.

Open your machine and look at the pin settings on the drives and check the IDE cables to determine which is the primary or secondary. Most CD devices have a set of six metal pins (two rows of three pins) located on the back of the drive. These pins are often labeled, telling you which two pins to put the jumper on to designate "master," "slave," or "cable select." Cable select means that the master or slave position will be determined by how the IDE cable is connected to the drives.

The reason for determining which devices are masters or slaves is that the new device will need to be installed as the one that is not taken. If your hard drive is the primary drive, then the CD device should be set to the secondary.

Once you have set the jumper, it is time to plug in your IDE cable and power cable into the drive, close up your tower and start your computer, making sure your computer sees the new drive. If your computer does not see the drive, try swapping the jumper to the opposite of what you originally set it, if you set it as a master, switch it to slave, and vice versa. Windows operating systems should see the drive without any special drivers, but most CD drives come with a driver just in case you are using a non-Windows operating system.

SCSI For SCSI drives, the procedure is similar, but on SCSI drives, you do not set a drive as master or slave; you must set it to a SCSI ID number. Most SCSI drives give you the jumper settings in the product documentation or on the drive. If you cannot find it, or you bought your drive OEM, then check the manufacturer's website.

17

DVD upgrade

You'll need a DVD upgrade kit, like the one from Hi-Val. It comes with everything you need to upgrade to a DVD system. It comes with a video card, an MPEG2 decoder, and a DVD drive. All you need to do is open the case, make sure you have mounting rails, and slide in the drive. If you don't have mounting rails you can buy them—they're cheap. Then, once you install the card and software you're good to go!

Before you upgrade, you should consider all the pros and cons of upgrading. There aren't actually a whole lot of reasons to upgrade to a DVD system right now. I mean, if you're going to be watching movies on DVD, you should just buy a DVD entertainment system so you can watch movies on your TV. The quality will be much better. Also, there aren't many DVD games out there right now. So, unless you have some really compelling reason to upgrade, you might want to consider waiting until prices go down and the companies start making more software that takes advantage of DVD technology.

If you believe the advertising hype, DVD is the latest must-have technology. So you might wonder, "If I don't buy a DVD drive, am I missing the boat? Are CD-ROMs going to go the way of the eight-track tape?" In short, the answer is no.

Depending on who you ask, DVD stands for either digital versatile disk or digital video disk. Storage capacity and data transfer rate are the most significant differences between CD-ROMs and DVD-ROMs. A DVD-ROM drive transfers data at a much faster rate than a CD-ROM drive; meaning that games and video will run faster and smoother from a DVD. And, while CD-ROMs can store up to 650 megabytes of data, a double-sided DVD-ROM can store a whopping 17 gigabytes of data—that's more than enough space to store a full-length movie with Dolby A-3 Digital Surround Sound!

CD-ROMs won't be going away anytime soon. But if you're a new-technology junkie, by all means, buy a DVD drive. Otherwise, there are good reasons why you should wait.

DVD is still expensive, and the technology still isn't fully developed. And, although you can play CD-ROMs in your DVD drive, it will still be a while before many titles are available on DVD.

On the other hand, there's never been a better time to buy a CD-ROM or a CD-RW drive. Prices are low, and if you buy a CD-ReWritable drive, you can use it for backing up and storing your data-something DVD can't do yet.

DVD stands for Digital Versatile Disk or Digital Video Disk, depending upon who you ask. A DVD-ROM drive is able to play video DVDs, data DVDs, data CDs and audio CDs. A DVD-RW is also able to write to a recordable DVD disk. DVD disks have a capacity of 4.7 gigabytes or the equivalent of three hours of video recording. A CD has a capacity of about 650 megabytes, less than 30 minutes of video.

DVD-ROM drives are slowly replacing CD-ROM drives because they are nearly the same price but you get the added capability to play DVDs. However DVD-RW drives are roughly six times more than CD-RW drives and the media is 20 times more expensive. Because of their capacity, DVDs will undoubtedly replace CDs as the media of choice as the prices decline.

DVD players in PCs are of limited use because most people don't want to watch movies on their PC monitor. The exception is for laptops, they make great entertainment centers while traveling.

These are some symptoms that may be caused by the DVD-ROM. Other components may also cause these same symptoms, check the general diagnosis page for more information.

I cannot access the drive and the light does not go on Check that the power and controller cables are securely attached to the drive.

Verify that pin #1 of the controller cable is matched to pin #1 on the drive and on the motherboard.

The operating system may not be configured to use or "see" the drive. If it never worked, verify that the jumpers on the drive are set correctly.

I cannot access the drive but the light does go on the disk may be damaged or unreadable. Try removing and reinserting the disk.

Try cleaning the disk. Verify that pin #1 of the controller cable is matched to pin #1 on the drive and on the motherboard. If it never worked, verify that the jumpers on the drive are set correctly.

The drive drawer will not open Press the button once and wait at least a minute. In Windows, go to "My Computer", right click on the DVD-ROM drive and choose "Eject" from the menu.

With the computer unplugged, you can open most DVD-ROM drawers with a unwound paper clip. Poke it, as straight as possible, into the hole and push with moderate force (the paper clip may bend a little) to force the drawer open a half inch. Now pull the drawer the rest of the way open. If the problem persists, check that the power connector and controller cable are securely connected to the drive.

A disk may be jammed or broken inside the drive. Access may require the removal of the drive's outer case. If this is necessary, it is very likely that the drive will have to be replaced.

I hear it spinning and then stopping repeatedly the disk may be damaged or unreadable.

Try removing and reinserting the disk.

Try cleaning the disk.

Verify that pin #1 of the controller cable is matched to pin #1 on the drive and on the motherboard. If it never worked, verify that the jumpers on the drive are set correctly.

The drive seems to transfer data too slowly is the drive on the same controller cable as the primary hard drive? If so, performance will be slowed because only one device can communicate at a time. Move it to the second IDE controller.

Before opening the case, unplug the PC

Static electricity is harmless to you but it can fry your computer chips. It's best to use a grounding strip or touch the metal frame of your case to complete the ground. This does not work as well but it is better to be safe then sorry.

Always follow the manufacturer's instructions if they deviate from our guide. Failure to do so may complicate the installation.

Unplug the PC

Open the case

If you are replacing a CD-ROM, disconnect the controller cable, power connector and audio connection (if present). Remove the retaining screws and remove the drive. Set the jumper to "Master" or "MA" if the drive will be the first or only drive on a controller. Set the jumper to "Slave" or "SL" if it will be the second drive on a controller. Insert the new drive into the bay used for the old drive, or select a bay that has a suitable corresponding opening in the case front. Make sure it is right side up (the button should be under the drawer). Secure the drive in place with the provided screws or rail inserts. Connect the controller cable to the drive and the motherboard (the second IDE controller is preferable). Make sure that pin #1 of the cable corresponds to pin #1 on the drive and motherboard. If you have two connectors to choose from, use the one at the end. Connect the power to the drive. Connect the audio wire (if one is being used) to the drive and to the sound card or motherboard. Close the case. Plug in the PC.

18

How do you install a Zip drive and use it?

Well it depends which kind of Zip drive you want to use. Iomega makes an assortment of drives that connect in different ways.

There are:

IDE Zip drives

SCSI Zip drives

Parallel port (printer port) Zip drives

USB Zip drives

IDE, SCSI, Parallel, and USB are the four different types of interfaces you can use to connect a drive to your computer. What's more, IDE and SCSI drives are available as internal or external drives.

There's also a product called Zip Plus. A Zip Plus can come with either a SCSI or a parallel port connection. Zip Plus is a little bit more expensive, but it's very flexible and can be a nice solution for many people.

Each kind of interface has its particular advantages and disadvantages. You need to decide which will work best for you.

Printer Port Zip:

A printer port Zip is the easiest kind to install and fairly simple to use. You can also move a printer port Zip drive easily from one machine to another. That means you can use a single Zip drive to back up multiple PCs. On the down side, a printer port Zip is not quite as fast as a SCSI or an IDE connection. It can also make it difficult to use your printer. You are supposed to plug your printer into the pass-through-port on the back of the Zip drive, and in some cases it works just fine—but not always. At the very least, you'll always have to have your Zip drive attached to the PC to be able to use your printer.

Internal IDE Zip

An internal IDE Zip is a little more difficult to install, but once you've got it set up, it and operates more quickly than a printer port Zip. Of course, it can only be installed on one machine. You can't move it from PC to PC. It's not quite as easy as installing the printer port Zip, but once you have it installed it's the simplest to use.

You'd install an internal Zip the same way you'd install a CD-ROM drive or an additional floppy drive. You'll have to have an open drive bay that has an opening in front. You'll slide the Zip drive in and connect it up to the IDE chain. Most computers can have up to 4 IDE devices, and most computers come with just 2—the CD-ROM drive and the hard drive—so often there's an extra space for an IDE Zip drive. That's how Leo has his Zip drive connected at home and at work. He has one Zip drive in each computer.

SCSI and USB Zips

SCSI port Zips are fast. If you have a SCSI card in your computer, you can either install a SCSI Zip drive by attaching it to the SCSI card internally or externally by attaching it to the SCSI board on the back of the PC.

USB Zip

The USB drive is the best and most sensible way of connecting a Zip to your PC. A plug-and-play USB Zip drive is the simplest to install and use. It provides the kind of speed you get with a SCSI connection, and—like other external drives—you can use it with more than one computer. Of course, your computer needs to have a USB port for you to be able to install one of these drives. A Zip drive appears just like the hard drive letter assignment (C: or D:) on your computer. A Zip drive is different because it's a removable disk. That means that the contents can vary just like the contents of a floppy can vary.

When you install the Zip software, you do need to know that it will make some modifications to your system. These modifications make sure that the Zip disk will eject when you shut your system down. When you insert a new disk, it will read and mount the new disk and open up a new window automatically.

What Can You Do With a Zip Drive?

You can copy files onto, and even run programs from your Zip drive. Keep in mind, however, that a Zip can only hold 100 megabytes. A Zip drive is really ideal for backing up critical files and for transferring files from one computer to another. If you get a new computer, we recommend that you buy either a Zip drive, or some other kind of high-density removable disk.

19

How do I install dual Video cards?

Just put them in and they'll work!

They need to both be the same kind of card. It won't work well if you have two cards from different manufacturers. Get two identical cards and they'll have instructions in the box on how to set it up. The driver is the same for the two cards, and what will happen is that the driver will tell one card to do one thing and the other card to do something else.

To set it up, you'll have to connect one card to the other, and connect the second one to your monitor. You'll have to turn on SLI (Scan Line Interleave) mode, which is the default, and is in the Control Panel for your card. It works quite nicely. In SLI mode, you can run Unreal—a very demanding game—in 1024x768. SLI mode will turn on automatically if there are two recognized cards.

I don't recommend dual Voodoo2 cards unless you have a Pentium II machine or better. PC Magazine found that dual Voodoo2 cards can actually slow down a computer that's not powerful enough to handle it.

One of the unique features of Voodoo2-based 3-D accelerator cards is their ability to work in tandem with a second Voodoo2 card, in order to split the 3-D rendering chores. This is a configuration known as Scan-Line Interleave (SLI) mode. When used in SLI mode, two

Voodoo2 cards render alternating scan lines on the screen: One card handles the even-numbered lines, and the other card handles the odd-numbered lines.

You might think this setup would double your performance, but it doesn't. The real benefit is that SLI mode lets you run games at higher resolutions without any significant degradation in performance. For example, a single Canopus Pure3D II card can run Quake II on our test system at about 68 frames per second in 640-by-480 resolution. At 800-by-600, the same card scores around 57 frames per second, and it is not even capable of running the game at 1,024-by-768. In SLI mode, two Pure3D II cards—the cards must be identical to work in SLI mode—can run the game at over 65 frames per second in 640-by-480, 800-by-600, and 1,024-by-768 resolutions.

As mentioned earlier, Voodoo2 is optimized for a Pentium II-based computer. This fact becomes glaringly obvious when you're using two Voodoo2 cards. In fact, it's not surprising to clock slower frame rates when using two cards in an MMX machine than when you've installed just one card. Pump up the CPU to, say; a 333-MHz PII and you'll see results. The focus of the SLI configuration is definitely games played at high resolution on a screaming-fast computer.

Since these are 3-D-only cards, you have to install them along with a basic 2-D or 2-D/3-D graphics card in order to use them. In other words, you need to free up three slots for graphics cards: one for your 2-D or 2-D/3-D card and two for the Video cards. You also will have to swallow the added expense of a second $75-plus Video card. Then again, you might be surprised by what some people will do just to be able to run Quake III at 70 frames per second in 1,024-by-768 resolution.

20

Raid

As processors, RAM, and video cards get better, the bottleneck is increasingly your hard drive. Unlike the days when you might have had one word processing file open, people today work with large media files and access the hard drive much more. So RAID makes a lot of sense. It's one area where The main idea in RAID is something called striping. Imagine two HD drives, one on top of another. Now take one sector in the top drive and one in the bottom drive. When you stripe data, the information is written across both sectors, across the drives, as if they were a single unit. The data is interleaved between both drives in an overlapping fashion. As a sector is read from the top drive, the read continues onto the bottom on an alternate sector.

What are the advantages? It depends which RAID level configuration you use. RAID levels have nothing to do with quality. A level 5 RAID isn't better than a level 1 RAID. Each level has different benefits. A quick breakdown:

RAID Level 0: Performs pure data striping, offering the ultimate in performance and drive efficiency. An oxymoron of sorts as it doesn't offer any level of redundancy whatsoever. Requires at least two drives.

RAID Level 1: Mirroring. This one duplicates data from one drive to the others within the array. It offers the same amount of storage as a single drive in the array but with complete data redundancy. Disable one drive and the others can still supply the data. A level 1 RAID writes slow compared to a single drive but makes up for it with faster reads. Choose this level for a high fault-tolerance environment. Requires at least two drives.

RAID Level 2: Offers the use of Hamming ECC (error correction code). It gives each bit an ECC and stores it on an ECC drive. When reading data, it checks against

The ECC drive(s) to verify data integrity. Of the five RAID levels this is the least used. It's an inefficient use of drives, costs a lot, and the Hamming ECC is irrelevant since SCSI and most new HDs support built-in error correction. Requires at least three drives.

RAID Level 3: Offers data striping at the bit level. It stores data parity on a parity disk with data correction on reads. You'll need a hardware controller for best results though, and controller design is complex. It's best for environments using long sequential data, like digital video editing. Not good in a multi-user situation. Requires at least three drives.

RAID Level 4: Similar to Level 3 except writes data at block level, not bit level. Its read performance is similar to Level 0. Level 4 writes much slower because the parity data must be updated at each write, although sequential or large writes are much faster. It offers low cost per mega-byte but makes for difficult data rebuild in event of disk failure. Little to no advantage over Level 5 with no support for multiple simulta-neous writes. Requires at least three hard drives.

RAID Level 5: Similar to Level 4 but with parity data distributed across all disks. Great in multi-user environments like file or Web serv-ers. Requires at least three hard drives, but better with five. What are the disadvantages? Number one is cost. You need at least two drives, and while you can use software, a hardware RAID controller offers bet-ter performance. Second, above Level 0, RAID uses valuable storage space for data redundancy. Complicated setups can mean significant downtime. And it can be just plain overkill. If all you do is surf the

Web and play the occasional 3D shooter there's really no need to spend the bucks for a RAID setup when you can send your kid to college instead.

Bootable floppy

You'll need to boot up your pristine new volume and prep it to receive all the data stored on your hard-drive backup CD. For details on creating a bootable floppy, read this

What is a boot disk?

A boot disk, or start-up disk, is what you start your computer with. You should recreate your boot disk whenever you make system changes such as installing new OS or adding new drivers. Everybody needs a boot disk.

To create a boot disk in Windows 98 and ME, follow these steps:

Insert a formatted floppy disk in your floppy drive.

Press Start.

Select Settings.

Select the Control Panel.

Double-click Add/Remove programs.

Click on the Startup Disk tab on the far right.

Press the "Create a Startup Disk" button and it will create a startup disk for you.

To start your computer using the boot disk, place the disk in the floppy drive as you turn your computer on.

What is an Emergency Recovery Utility (ERU)?

ERU is not the same as a boot disk. The ERU saves critical information onto the hard drive. It's used to back up files in case of damage to your system. You can also save the ERU to a floppy, but it's not really worth the time it would take to transfer that much data.

ERU is hidden and isn't always installed on Windows, but it is on the Windows installation disk. Microsoft hides it because it considers this feature to be for tech-support people only.

More advanced computer users may want to install ERU—it's only found on your Windows 95 installation CD.

Go to the Windows 95 CD directory named other/Misc.

Drag and copy the folder named ERU to your Drive C:/(or other hard drive of choice).

Double-click the new ERU folder on your hard drive.

In the ERU directory, locate the file ERU.inf.

Right-click on the ERU.inf file.

Click install on the menu that pops up.

Media for backing up your hard drive

Unless you're setting up a RAID 1 array designed to simply mirror what's on the drive you already have, everything on your current hard drive will be gone-daddy-gone if you don't back it up first. This is a good practice even if you're not planning to set up a RAID array, since it protects you against unforeseen disasters.

IDE hard drives

How many hard drives you need depends on the array you're setting up, but two is the minimum. Remember, your array will only perform as well as your smallest and slowest drive. For a RAID that rocks, build an array that's made of identically equipped drives.

Hardware controller

Since you'll need to choose a controller that matches your hard drives' ATA speed, your options will be determined by the drives going into your array.Set Up an IDE RAID Array Connect the RAID controller to the hard drives using standard 80-pin cabling. When using two drives, place each drive on its own ATA channel. For a four-drive configuration, attach two drives to each ATA channel.

Set the hard drives' jumpers according to the number of drives in the array. In a two-drive setup, both drives should be set as Masters. In a four-drive setup, each channel should house one Master and one Slave each.

Seat the controller in an open PCI slot. Install the hard drives. Attach their power supplies and seat them inside your case.

Boot the PC. Before your BIOS screen appears, you'll find yourself in your hardware controller's utility program. A message should say "Array is undefined," and your computer will ask you to do some configuring. You'll see options such as "Set type of array" (striped, mirrored, and so on). Choose the options you want.

Insert bootable floppy in disk drive and reboot.

Use the fdisk utility to set partitions on the array, then format the volume to your liking.

Load your spanking new hard drive with the backup image you stored on a CD.

Monitor your array to your heart's content. The monitoring utility that came with your controller will report all of your array's vital statistics, such as size, RAID level, and so on.

21

How to install a hard drive

Almost everybody should buy an EIDE hard drive.

You will save yourself money, hassle, and really won't lose out on performance. Get a big, 7200-rpm EIDE drive. It will be fast enough, and the price is so much less per megabyte than a comparable SCSI drive. Use that extra change to get a faster processor or more RAM, both of which will show you a far bigger performance boost than that SCSI drive.

Unplug the PC

Static electricity is harmless to you but it can fry your computer chips. Static electricity is mainly caused by dry air and or friction e.g., dragging your feet across a carpet. It's best to use a grounding strip. Or touch the metal frame of your case to complete the ground before you unplug it. This does not work as well but it is better to be safe then sorry. To lower the risk of static electricity, avoid standing on carpet. Ideally, you should have your computer set up on a grounding mat. Consult your manual if you need help opening your computer's case.

This isn't as scary as it sounds. In fact, you can be up and running with a shiny new hard drive in less than an hour. The sky's the limit. Well, actually your bank account is the limit on a brand new one. The hard drive doesn't have to be brand new, though; you can also install an old one that you have lying around. It does have to work correctly, however.

Before you open the case on your computer, make sure your computer is completely unplugged from the wall. Only after you've unplugged should you open it up. Consult your manual if you need help opening your computer's case.

Once you've opened up the case, it's time to inspect the components. You want to double-check that you have an extra space in which to insert the new hard drive, an extra spot on the IDE ribbon that's connected to the other hard drive on your system, and an additional four-prong female power supply adapter. Most computers have ample room for additional hardware. Look directly under or below your current drive. There should be an empty spot to slide a new drive into. The IDE ribbon is always gray and has a width of about two inches. Sometimes the gray ribbon will have a blue or red strip. The ribbon that's connected to your current hard drive is considered the primary IDE. On the primary IDE ribbon, look for an identical connector like the one that's already connected to your current drive. This connector is the one you'll use to attach to your new drive. Follow all the cords coming from your power supply. All you need to find is one four-prong female power adapter. Most computers have one or two extras to support additional drives (CD-ROM, floppy, hard drive). This power adapter is what you'll use to supply power to your new hard drive.

Master or Slave?

When using more than one hard drive on a computer, it is required that one drive be designated a master and the other a slave before they're installed. The term master applies to whichever hard drive your computer boots from or hard drive where your OS is stored. The term slave refers to any secondary hard drive that's connected to your system.

Before installing your new hard drive, take a look at the top of the drive. On it you should see a diagram for setting the jumper. The diagram should depict different sets of pins with a black box around two of them. Locate the diagram for changing the jumper setting to a slave.

To change the jumper, you may need to have a set of tweezers handy. Use them to reposition the jumper between the four male prongs and the IDE ribbon connector. Match the settings depicted in the diagram on top of the hard drive to make sure you do this correctly.

You may want to make sure your original hard drive jumper is set to a master. Chances are it already is since most hard drives come this way. You should double-check just to be sure.

To install the new drive:

With the power supply still unplugged, place the new drive into its available location.

Mount the drive to the computer by screwing two screws on both sides of the chassis.

Connect the four-prong power supply to the back of the hard drive.

Connect the IDE ribbon to the back of the hard drive.

Remove all screwdrivers and additional screws from inside the case before closing it.

Close the case.

Insert your computer's plug back into its power supply.

Now, turn you computer on.

When you turn your computer on, it should automatically detect the new drive. Watch it as it boots up. Look as it finds a primary IDE master and another labeled primary IDE slave. The master and the slave should have the manufacturer's serial number next to each of them.

If it doesn't recognize the new drive, then you'll need to go into the BIOS to designate the new drive as a primary IDE slave. Please consult your manual for guidelines on doing this.

Now, it's time to partition the new drive.

The best way to do this and the easiest is to use third party software. You can download free from the Internet. Like E-Z Install the best get it at **http://www.westerndigital.com/support/download/**

EZ-Install is a self-extracting file that creates a bootable diskette that runs only the EZ-Install portion of the DLG Tools. This version of EZ-Install is part of DLG Tools. Just download unzips to 3-2 inch disk. Restart your computer with disk in drive and follow the on screen directions. It does all the work for you.

Or windows come with a built-in utility called fdisk. This program is used to partition a large hard drive into smaller virtual drives. One advantage of having two smaller virtual drives is the decreased downtime while running applications such as ScanDisk or Defrag.

To use fdisk to partition a hard drive, follow these directions:

To open fdisk, left-click the Start menu, select Run or Hold, and release the Windows button+R.

At the command line, type "fdisk" (without quotes) and hit Enter.

When fdisk opens you'll be asked if you'd like to enable large disk support. "Y" should already be selected. Hit Enter.

Next, you need to set the current fixed disk drive to equal your newly installed hard drive. To do this, select 5 from the list and press Enter.

Find the number next to your new drive, type it into Enter Fixed Disk Drive Number, and hit Enter. (In most cases, if you just added a second hard drive, the number from the list will equal 2. Before you proceed, double-check that the current fixed hard drive is equal to the new hard drive you just installed. If it is, you should see any number other than 1 next to Current Fixed Drive.)

This will take you back to the beginning screen.

From here, select 1 to "Create DOS Partition or Logical DOS Drive" and hit Enter.

Select 1 to "Create Primary DOS Partition" and hit Enter.

Your computer will begin to verify the new drive's integrity. This process will only take few minutes to complete. The next screen to appear will ask, "Do you wish to use the maximum available size for a Primary DOS partition?" Press Y if you only want to create one partition or N if you'd like to create multiple partitions on the drive. Then hit Enter.

Create one partition

If you pressed Y, the computer will create the partition and then transfer you back to the beginning screen. From here, select 4 to inspect to new hard drive's partition.

Create multiple partitions

If you pressed N, then you're going to create multiple partitions. To do this, you'll need to set the size of the new partition. This is done by entering a value next to "Enter partition size in Mbytes or percent of disk space to create a Primary DOS Partition."

For example, if your new hard drive is 20GB and you'd like to create two 10GB drives, entering 50% will do just fine. To enter a number in Mbytes, take the total number in Mbytes and divide it in half to get the correct number to input. To make things easier, just use a percentage of the total hard drive and let your computer do the math for you.

When you've finished entering the size of the new partition, hit Enter to create it.

Press Esc to return to the new drives main menu.

From here, select 1 to "Create DOS Partition or Logical DOS Drive."

Now it's time to create the extended partition. To do this, select 2 from the menu and hit Enter.

A screen that says "Enter partition size in Mbytes or percent of disk space to create an Extended DOS Partition" will appear. You should notice that the computer did the math for you and filled in the remaining hard drive space to be partitioned. If this number is OK, press Enter to complete the process. If it's not, and you plan on creating additional partitions, lower the number accordingly and then press Enter.

After fdisk creates the partition, press Esc to return to the new hard drive's main menu.

Before the new extended partition will work, it needs to have a Logical DOS Drive created on it. To do this, select 1 on the list to "Create DOS Partition or Logical DOS Drive."

Select 3 from the list to "Create Logical DOS Drive(s) in the Extended DOS Partition" and hit Enter.

Your computer will then verify drive integrity and automatically deliver the size of the extended drive. You should see a number next to

"Enter logical drive size in Mbytes or percentage of drive." This number should equal the size of the extended drive you created earlier.

Press Enter to "Create Logical DOS Drive(s) in the Extended DOS Partition."

After hitting Enter, you'll see a new letter assigned to the new partition you just created.

Press Esc to exit this screen and return to main menu.

How many partitions do you have?

To verify the two new partitions were created successfully, select 5 to "Change current fixed disk drive" and hit Enter.

You should see all the drives on your computer, including the two you just created.

Hit Esc twice to exit fdisk.

You must restart your computer before the new partitions will be recognized.

Format Your New Drive

Now that your computer recognizes the new drive, or drives depending on how many partitions you created, all that's left to do is format them before they're ready for use.

Since anti-virus programs won't allow anything to modify the master boot record, it's important to disable them before you proceed to formatting your new hard drive(s).

To format your new hard drive(s), follow these directions:

Double-click My Computer or press and release the Windows button+E.

You should see an additional drive with letter the D: and a possible third with the letter E: (if you created multiple partitions).

Right-click your new D: drive and select Format from the list.

Next, change the Format Type to Full.

Press the Start button to begin formatting the drive. Follow the directions above to finish formatting any remaining partitions you may have created on your new hard drive.

22

How to partition your Hard Drive

Changing your hard disk partitions can be frightening since it may involve data loss. Here's what you need to know before you start. If you were to compile a list of your favorite rainy day activities, it's a good bet that partitioning your hard disk wouldn't be among them. If you're like most people—novices and veterans alike—the very idea of partitioning is terrifying. Once you delete a partition, there is no turning back, so you must be absolutely certain of what you're doing before you begin.

If you delete a partition, you not only delete all data in it, but you also render that part of your hard disk inaccessible to your operating system. So if your hard disk consists of only one partition. As the disks in most new computers do, then deleting the partition would mean that you couldn't access your drive at all, not even if you were to boot from your emergency floppy disk (you've made one, right?).

If you've made up your mind to modify your partitions, be sure to make a complete backup before you use any disk-partitioning utility. DOS and Windows 95 include a small program called FDISK, which until a few years ago was the only readily available utility for creating and deleting partitions. To access the utility, type "fdisk" at the DOS prompt and press Enter. A small menu, from which you can get all your partition information, will pop up. Move around the menu to your heart's content, but for safety's sake you should avoid item 3,

"Delete partition of Logical DOS Drive." FDISK runs you through several confirmations before deleting a partition, but why take the chance? On the other hand, item 1—"Create DOS partition or Logical DOS Drive"—tells you several things about your hard disk without destroying anything. You may even discover free space you never knew you had.

Taking a hard disk from its pristine, newly manufactured state to a fully functional DOS or Windows 95 storage area requires three steps: physical formatting, partitioning, and logical formatting. To understand what each step does, let's take a brief look at how hard disks operate.

Hard disks are mechanical devices consisting of several stacked platters (small, round metal disks treated to store magnetic charges on both sides), a spindle around which the platters rotate (much like the center post on a record turntable), and read and write heads attached to the disks by a mechanical arm. The read and write heads allow magnetic charges to be stored on the disk (as bits) and retrieved from it. When you direct a program to load a file from the disk, the platters spin around the spindle and the read head moves back and forth over the platters until it locates the desired bits. Software in the hard disk and the hard disk controller then loads the bits into RAM. When you save data, your computer transfers a series of bits to the hard disk, recorded by the write heads as magnetic charges.

From the standpoint of your computer, the hard disk is completely useless until it undergoes the formatting and partitioning stages. The first of these stages is physical or low-level formatting, which in most cases is handled by the manufacturer (older drives and SCSI drives have utilities that refresh low-level formats, but IDE drives don't). Low-level formatting essentially gives the disk its physical structure. It adds tracks, sectors, and cylinders, terms with which you're familiar if you've ever had the pleasure of installing a new hard disk.

You can think of tracks as being like the grooves on a long-playing record, although tracks are laid out in separate concentric circles rather than one long, continuous spiral like the grooves on an LP. Tracks are divided into sectors, each of which can store a given amount of data, and each platter has its own tracks and sectors. A cylinder encompasses all the platters comprising the corresponding track—that is, the track that is the same distance from the spindle—on each. To visualize cylinders, think of a tall stack of pancakes and a number of drinking glasses, each having a different diameter. Center a glass above the pancakes, and then push down right through the entire stack. Then do the same with each remaining glass. The vertical configurations you've produced are cylinders.

Once a hard disk has been physically formatted, it can be divided into physical regions called partitions. Each partition occupies a group of contiguous cylinders and with some operating systems (Linux, for example), you can specify precisely which cylinders you want each partition to occupy. The purpose behind partitioning is to segment your hard disk, for organization's sake and also to let you run multiple operating systems on a single computer. Each operating system works best (and sometimes solely) with its own file system, and only one file system can exist in a single partition. Under some file systems, there's a third reason for multiple partitions: to cut down on wasted space. We'll deal with all these reasons a little later in this article.

Even with your partitions in place, the hard disk is still useless to your computer. To make each partition capable of storing information, it must be logically formatted. Where physical formatting gives your disk its physical structure, logical formatting (which is unrelated to physical formatting) provides a means of exchanging data with the operating system by giving the disk a logical structure, the file system. When you use the FORMAT command in DOS or the Format menu item in Windows Explorer, you are initiating a logical format of either a floppy disk or a hard disk.

The sole purpose of logical formatting is to place a file system on the disk. Your operating system determines what file system is available to you; you rarely get a choice. The most common file systems for machines driven by Intel processors are:

FAT (File Allocation Table)—the standard file system for DOS and Windows. Because of its widespread use, FAT is also accessible by Linux, OS/2, Windows NT, and other operating systems.

VFAT (Virtual File Allocation Table)—a protected-mode version of the FAT file system, used by Windows 95. It is compatible with the FAT system, the main difference being support for long filenames.

NTFS (NT File System)—Windows NT's native file system. You can install Windows NT on a FAT partition, but NTFS is far more advanced, with better security and reliability, faster file access, and very little wasted space.

HPFS (High Performance File System)—OS/2's native file system. As with NTFS, which evolved from HPFS, the security, reliability, speed, and efficiency are far superior to FAT's.

FAT32 (32-bit File Allocation Table)—included with Windows 95 OSR2, a version that is only available preinstalled by the system manu-facturer. FAT32 gets rid of many FAT limitations. But so far, it can't be accessed by anything other than Win95 OSR2.

After logical formatting, a partition is also known as a volume. shows the file systems on a drive volume. It's a good idea to give volume names to your partitions, which you can do through DOS's LABEL command or with Windows Explorer. Naming your partitions will make them easier to recognize when you use partitioning software such as FDISK, reducing the risk of destroying the wrong partition

If you've played with FDISK at all, you're probably familiar with pri-mary, extended, and logical partitions. Primary and extended are major partition types, and the total number you can have on your hard disk is limited. You can divide each hard disk into as many as four major partitions, and only one of those can be an extended partition.

Note that these limitations have nothing to do with the operating system. They stem from a decision, made by drive and BIOS manufacturers in the early years of hard disks, that four partitions should be enough for anyone (a bit like DOS's 640K memory limit). The extended partition was developed in response to the need for more than four partitions. An extended partition can itself be divided into as many logical partitions as you wish; in a sense, the extended partition acts as a container for them. In a system with multiple operating systems, it's common to have a primary partition for each OS and an extended partition, subdivided into three or four logical partitions, for the OS you use most frequently. In the DOS/Windows 95/Windows NT world, drive letters are assigned according to partition type. When your computer boots, it checks the master boot record, which is usually on the first sector of the first disk, and reads the partition table in that record. The partition table tells the computer how the disks are partitioned, and the operating system assigns letters accordingly. The designations A: and B: are reserved for floppy disk drives, and the active primary partition (only one can be active) on the first hard disk is assigned C:. Now the first primary partition on each additional hard disk gets the next letter, in sequence. Once the primary partitions on all hard disks have been assigned letters, all the logical partitions on the first hard disk take their turn, followed by all the logical partitions on the second disk, and so on. If you add a new hard disk to a single-drive system that had volumes designated C: and D:, the new disk's primary partition becomes D: and your old D: becomes E:. Note that the OS will assign letters only to partitions it recognizes, so DOS/Windows 95 will ignore an NTFS partition.

Most new computers are shipped with a large (1GB or greater) hard disk with only one partition. This causes three potential problems.

First, it makes it hard to organize your programs and data, because you end up filling the C: drive with so many directories that finding anything becomes difficult. Wouldn't it make more sense to have a partition for programs, another for data and downloads, a third for games, and so on? Second, if you want to install an additional OS and want to use the file system native to that OS, you'll have to back up your entire hard disk, delete the existing partition and create new ones, then reformat and reinstall the operating system, programs, and data from scratch. In other words, not likely.

The third problem might come as a surprise. Large FAT partitions waste disk space. That may not seem logical—one big building with multiple rooms seems more efficient than several smaller buildings—but it's true. The problem stems from the fact that the FAT file system was developed in the days when floppy disks ruled and hard disks were small, and it was never meant to scale onto today's multigigabyte drives. It's extremely inefficient at storing files. Why? To put it simply, FAT divides its partitions into groupings of sectors called clusters. That's fine, except that FAT also limits the number of clusters in a given partition to just over 65,000. As a result, as the size of the partition grows, so does the size of each cluster. For a partition under 128MB, for example, each cluster will be 2K in size, while a partition between 1GB and 2GB has a relatively huge cluster size of 32K. And it's not as if you have a choice; that 32K cluster size is the minimum for a 1GB partition, again because of the limited number of clusters the partition can have.

FAT allocates disk space to files using whole clusters, even though very few files are precise multiples of the cluster size. The data occupying a file's last cluster may fill the cluster completely, or it may be as little as a single byte. With an even distribution of file sizes, the average wasted space per file will be half a cluster. On a 127MB drive with 2K clusters, your CONFIG.SYS file, typically about 0.5K in size, wastes 1.5K. The same file on a 1.2GB drive with 32K clusters wastes 31.5K. On that same 1.2GB drive, a 100K file occupies just over three 32K clusters, with the majority of the fourth cluster remaining empty. The chart below shows roughly how much wasted space you can expect.

Partition Size and Probable Waste

Partition size	Cluster size	Avg. waste per file	Number of files	Probable waste
Less than 128MB	2K	1K	2,000	2MB
128 to 256MB	4K	2K	4,000	8MB
256 to 512MB	8K	3K	8,000	32MB
512MB to 1GB	16K	8K	16,000	128MB
1GB to 2GB	32K	16K	32,000	512MB

As the table clearly shows, small partitions mean less wasted space. It's a no-brainer, then, right? Fire up FDISK and go to it. But as we've already discussed, that's a lot of work. Who has a couple of evenings to spend backing up and restoring data and reinstalling programs?

That's where third-party partitioning software comes in. The most common packages are Power Quest's Partition Magic and Quarterdeck's Partition-It, both of which do much the same thing. Their primary role is to let you change the size of a partition without destroying the data in it, but they can do much more. Each package also includes a utility for moving applications from one partition to another, adjusting system references as necessary. At first, they're a bit terrifying for FDISK veterans, who tend to think of partitioning as destroying data, but they work well.

I used Partition Magic extensively while researching this article. The program analyzes your partitions and calculates wasted space and lets you resize and move your partitions by sliding your mouse pointer along a bar. It works with FAT, FAT32, NTFS, and HPFS partitions, and it lets you resize clusters on the fly. It even deals with changed drive letters by remapping system references to existing applications. Its most impressive moment, however, comes after you've completed your work, when it tells you how much of your hard disk you've reclaimed.

23

How to Install a New CPU

If you're putting together your own computer and you're stressing over placing the processor in the motherboard, calm down. There is nothing to worry about here. Installing a CPU is a pretty straightforward process.

Most of the damage that occurs during this process comes from doing it carelessly or using the wrong heat sink. So take your time and be gentle.

Here's how to do it:

Open the ZIF socket. Lift the lever by pulling slightly to the side (this releases the lock) and then up to vertical.

Insert the CPU. Most processors use a zero insertion force (ZIF) socket, which means exactly that. If there is any resistance, stop. The weight of the chip should be more than enough to fit the processor into the socket. Check to make sure everything is aligned properly. The pins should be laid out in such a way that they will only go in one way. Carefully look to make sure no pins are bent.

Close the ZIF socket. Double check that the CPU is lying flat on the socket and then push the lever down to its horizontal position, where it will lock in place. Some resistance here is normal (some, not a lot).

Install the heat sink/fan

Make sure you have the correct heat sink/fan for your type of CPU (it will specify which type of CPU it is for). If you don't have the packing or are not completely sure, you are better off buying a new heat sink/fan than a new CPU.

Align the fan properly. There is one side of the socket that will have a wider gap between the CPU and the edge of the socket. Make sure this is in the same orientation on the heat sink/fan.

Make sure you have heat sink compound on the heat sink. This is very important.

Lay the heat sink/fan on the CPU. Clip one side on and carefully press the other clip down. If necessary you might have to use a screwdriver to carefully help get the second clip on.

Plug the fan in.

24

The Cooling Fan

A PC generates a lot of heat and heat is a major enemy of electronics. So it is important to keep your PC running cool. Most PCs employ a combination of heat sinks and fans. All power supplies incorporate a fan. Most CPUs have an attached fan. Many PCs have another fan inside the case to circulate air and some have fans just for cooling the drives. Because these fans have moving parts and they always run while the computer is on, they will wear out. It is not uncommon for a fan to wear out in just one year, although many run for years. If a fan in your PC stops running, it is critical that it be replaced. Your PC will run without an operating fan, but possibly not for long. It is never wise to run the PC if there is a possibility of overheating. Fortunately, fans are inexpensive and relatively easy to replace.

How to Diagnose Cooling Fan Problems

These are some symptoms that may be caused by the cooling fans. Other components may also cause these same symptoms, check the general diagnosis page for more information.

It makes a squealing or other loud noise the power supply fan is failing and needs replacement. In most cases, the entire power supply must be replaced. The CPU fan is failing and needs replacement. Another cooling fan, such as a case, drive or auxiliary fan is failing and needs replacement.

The fan is slow or does not spin at all the power supply fan is failing and needs replacement. In most cases, the entire power supply must be replaced. The CPU fan is failing and needs replacement. Another cooling fan, such as a case, drive or auxiliary fan is failing and needs replacement.

The PC freezes or shuts itself off unexpectedly the system may be overheating because of inadequate cooling. Check that all cooling fans are working properly.

25

Install power a new supply

How to Diagnose Power Supply Problems

These are some symptoms that may be caused by the power supply. Other components may also cause these same symptoms, check the general diagnosis page for more information.

It makes a squealing or other loud noise the power supply fan is failing and needs replacement. In most cases, the entire power supply must be replaced.

Nothing happens when I turn on the PC Check that it is securely plugged into the outlet and into the back of the PC.

Check that the outlet has power. Check for a second power switch near the power supply. The main power switch has failed and needs to be replaced. The power supply has failed and needs to be replaced.

The PC freezes before the operating system starts loading if the power supply does not supply the proper, stable voltages to the various components it may prevent the PC from starting. The voltages can be tested with a millimeter.

The PC randomly shuts itself off the power supply could be overheating, check that the fan is working. The power supply could be failing. See also your BIOS and Control Panel power settings.

How to install and new power supply.

Static electricity is harmless to you but it can fry your computer chips. It's best to use a grounding strip or touch the metal frame of your case to complete the ground. This does not work as well.

Unplug the power supply from the wall. Unplug the peripheral power cables.

Unplug the power cable from the motherboard. Make sure to pinch the tab that is located on the side of the plug, and wiggle the connector if needed.

Remove the screws on the back of the case that hold the power supply in. Slide the power supply out of the case.

Reverse the process to put it back together.

Make sure the voltage is set to 110 (a little red recessed switch on the back of the power supply). It is typically set here by default.

Depending on the power supply you have, it may have an on/off switch on the back as well.

26

How to Identify Chips on the Motherboard

First, you get a job with a chip manufacturer, like Intel. After a couple years making chips in the lab, you'll be able to identify them all, no sweat. You'll get to wear a funky bunny suit too.

But seriously, identifying the chips inside a PC case is tough, even for professionals. Often you can't definitively identify them, only deduce their type by size and location. Here are some clues:

Central processor or CPU

he easiest chip to identify is the largest chip on the motherboard; that's the central processor. It should have a ceramic heat sync glued to it. If there's not a heat sync glued to it you can actually look at the chip and see what it is. Looking for numbers like 80486, Pentium, Pentium II, and K6—that kind of thing. You may or may not find numbers that give you an idea of chip's clock speed.

Chip set

The next biggest chip is the chip set. The chips set are also referred to as the bridge chips, the logic chips or the glued chips. Nowadays, on most modern motherboards, the chip set is a single chip. If the motherboard is over a couple of years old it might be two chips. Sometimes the chip set is labeled Intel, or with the name of another manufacturer. Common chip set manufacturers include VIA, SIS, and ALI. The chip set contains controllers for the memory, the PCI bus, and your peripheral cards among other things.

Cache RAM

Often, the hardest chips to find on the motherboard are the cache RAM chips. They are usually soldered into the motherboard. They're often quite small and not obviously memory. Look around for small microprocessors. There may be four or six or two—not very many.

RAM chips

There are two ways of attaching chips to circuit boards; surface mounting which means that the chip is soldered right onto the board, and socketed, which means a chip socket is soldered into the board and a chip is inserted into the sockets.

The RAM chips are rarely attached to the motherboard directly. They're almost always in RAM sockets—usually perpendicular to the motherboard on smaller circuit boards called sticks. SIMM sticks or DIMM sticks are small green circuit boards with chips attached.

Jumper ability? What's that? Most recent PC motherboards use jumpers. Jumpers are "metal bridges that close an electrical circuit. Typically, a jumper consists of a plastic plug that fits over a pair of protruding pins. Jumpers are sometimes used to configure expansion boards. By placing a jumper plug over a different set of pins, you can change a board's parameters." In this way the board can be configured for a differing set of parameters for the clock multiplier and the bus clock respectively.

The clock multiplier sets the speed of the CPU as a ratio of the bus clock. For example, the bus clock of most Pentium machines is 66 MHz. Say you've got a Pentium 200MMX—that means your clock multiplier is set to three. (3 x 66 MHz=200 MHz).

This means you can get a Socket 7 CPU from Intel up to 233MMX or a non-Intel CPU that can go up to 300 (such as the AMD K6-2) if your motherboard's clock multiplier can be set to 4.5 (4.5 x 66 MHz=300 MHz). Check your motherboard manual for the exact settings.

However, if you want to get the best possible speed, it would be better to get a new motherboard—a Super Socket 7 or Slot 1 (i.e. Pentium II). Super Socket 7 is a new form factor for CPUs that supports a 100-MHz bus (the original Pentium only went up to 66 MHz) as a reaction against Intel's patenting its Slot 1 technology. Super Socket 7 is an enchanted form factor of the Socket 7 CPU form (Pentium MMX CPUs). Currently, AMD holds the title for the fastest CPUs in this form factor.

Slot 1 is what Pentium IIs and Celerons use. It was a way to place the L2 cache (in the Pentium II and Celeron A) closer to the CPU core to increase speed. Regular Pentiums placed the L2 cache on the motherboard. Slot 1s look like rectangular cartridges.

27

Install a New Motherboard

Steps for installing a motherboard

Unplug the PC

Static electricity is harmless to you but it can fry your computer chips. It's best to use a grounding strip or touch the metal frame of your case to complete the ground. This does not work as well but it is better to be safe then sorry.

Open the case.

Take a close look at its innards. Lay your new motherboard next to the case in the same alignment as the motherboard the case.

Notice where all the cables go

Keep track of your cables

Feel nervous? You could label each cable as you pull it out of the system with a piece of masking tape, noting which side of the cable is pin one, and so on. Many of the cables, such as the power cable, can only go into their sockets in one direction. The IDE cables for the hard drive are the most annoying ones, so pay close attention to them. Once you're comfortable with the cable soup carry on.

Remove all the cards, cables, and memory from the old motherboard. You should now have clear access to all the screws or clips that holds the old motherboard. Remove them.

Look all around the motherboard for one last screw or clip. I always miss one of 'em in the clutter. Gently pull the motherboard clear from the back of the case where all the ports stick out, then pull it up. If you're lucky, neither the power supply nor the hard drive cage will block the motherboard egress. (If they do, you'll need to pull them out too.) Grab the new motherboard and do the above steps in reverse.

28

Building the new PC

Building the new PC-Catching up on Technology the New Motherboards

Socket 423 and Socket 478

Slot A

Slot 1 and Slot 2

Socket A

Super 7 and Socket 370

Socket 7, Socket 8

ATX (AT eXtension) Specification

ATX Motherboards

ATX Cases

ATX Power Supplies

New CPU Features

Intel Pentium 4

AMD Athlon

Intel Pentium III

AMD Duron

Intel Pentium II

Intel Celeron

Intel Pentium PRO

Intel Pentium MMX

Intel Pentium

AMD K6-3

AMD K6-2

AMD K6

AMD K5 PRxx

Cyrix MediaGX

Cyrix MII

Cyrix 6x86 MMX

Cyrix 6x86

Cache Memory

The Memory Bus

DRAM (Dynamic Random Access Memory)

FPM (Fast Page Memory)

EDO (Extended Data Out)

SDRAM Synchronous DRAM

DDR (Double Data Rate)

RAMBUS RIMM

Parity and ECC RAM

Drive Basics

Drive Interfaces and Performance-IDE and SCSI

EIDE and Fast ATA

SCSI

DVD

56K Modems-USR x2, k56flex and V.90

The Video Subsystem

A lot has changed since the mix and match days of the 486 clones. Today, just choosing which CPU to go with, from Intel or AMD, locks in the choice of motherboard, adapters, even power supply. Upgrading older PCs with state-of-the-art motherboards is rarely cost effective these days, a new hard drive, RAM and video card are practically required, and if you include a new CD, you may as well just buy a new 3.5" floppy drive for $15, another $30 to $70 for the case of your choice, and give a friend (or enemy) your old clunker. This page is sort of a scratchpad what I want to remember to include in my books. My "Build Your Own PC" series for McGraw-Hill is now in its second edition, and includes Athlon and Pentium III. For a pictorial approach to building an ATX PC (online example is a Pentium II from the first book), see the Illustrated Guide to Building the New PCs.

The New Motherboards

When it comes to PC repairs and upgrades, the greatest evolutionary step between generations of hardware occurred around 1994/1995, when the highly integrated motherboard became standard equipment. Integrated motherboards existed well before then, but the cost difference between a standard motherboard and a highly integrated one amounted to much more than the cost of the adapter cards replaced. Also, many early integrated motherboards really included the wrong adapters, such as a limited capability SVGA port or outdated SCSI connector. Motherboard manufacturers finally figured out that the most important adapter to get on the motherboard was the SIDE card, which included the floppy controller, a two device IDE (Intelligent Drive Electronics) controller, two serial ports, a parallel port (commonly called the printer port), and a game controller port. A secondary IDE channel capable of supporting an additional 2 IDE drives was soon made standard, along with the software upgradeable BIOS (Basic Input Output System). The new BIOS software usually supported Plug-n-Play devices, auto detection of hard drive parameters, and support for larger hard drives. One of the more recent additions that may become standard is onboard 16bit SoundBlaster compatible support. High end motherboards may integrate everything from SVGA, modem and Ethernet adapter to Fast SCSI and RAID (Redundant Array of Inexpensive Drives), but I would tend to avoid locking myself in to these rapidly evolving technologies on the motherboard level. The plugs in adapters are generally less expensive, and can be easily upgraded.

Socket 423 and Socket 478

Socket 423, named for its 423 pins, is the original Pentium 4 socket. Socket 478 is the successor to 423, supporting new sizes and speeds of the P4. While current P4s only support Rambus RIMM for high performance or the old PC133 memory for slower systems, support for

266MHz DDR should be available by the first quarter of 2002. The P4 is not available in a slot format.

Slot A

Slot A was developed by Digital Equipment (now a division of Compaq) for their Alpha processor, which was running a 1GHz a couple years ago. Therefore, Slot A actually has a history and is exceptionally stable for a newly introduced technology-at least as far as the consumer PC world goes. Slot A supports the new AMD Athlon, at speeds from 500 MHz to 800 MHz. However, support for the Athlons 266MHz front side bus (FSB) appeared in the Fall of 2000 when AMD introduces it's new chipsets that support DDR (Double Data Rate) SDRAM. AMD is phasing out Slot A in favor of Socket A.

Slot 1 and Slot 2

In the late 1990's, Intel decided that the best way to increase performance (and market share) was to abandon the Socket type CPU design which had been continually in use since the early 1980's and move to a edge connected, or slot form CPU. The slot form allows for a much larger CPU package, which usually includes tightly coupled cache to boost CPU performance. The Intel Pentium II was the first of these slot type CPUs, utilizing Slot 1, and was soon followed by the Pentium II Xeon, which used the non-compatible Slot 2. However, in order to compete in lower cost, easier to manufacture systems, Intel returned to the Socket for with Socket 370, and both the Pentium III and Celeron are now available in Socket 370 form.

Socket A

Socket A is the most recent addition to the standard CPU socket family. AMD is currently the only manufacturer of Socket A CPUs, these being the Athlon and the Duron. Socket a CPUs are somewhat less expensive than their Slot A brethren, due to the smaller package and reduced amount of cache memory integrated with the CPU. AMD warns that Socket A CPUs should not be used with adapters as Slot A CPUs.

Super 7

Super 7 basically refers to Socket 7 type motherboards that support a 100MHz bus and AGP. The Super 7 motherboards I have seen are ATX boards (see main FAQ), with the I/O core on the motherboard, so you can't stuff them in old cases. Super 7 motherboards may be equipped with as much as 2MB of L3 cache, which the newer AMD CPUs can access at 100MHz. The clock rates on these new AMD CPUs are up to 450MHz.

Socket 370

Intel has decided to take it's Celeron CPU back into competition in the PGA (Pin Grid Array) Socket world, in parallel with continuing to produce it as a Slot 1 device. Socket 370, so named for its 370 pin grid, is NOT compatible with Socket 7 or Super 7, it just looks similar. The Pentium III is now also available for Socket 370, but make sure your Socket 370 motherboard can handle a 100MHz or 133MHz bus before wasting a FCPGA (Flip Chip Pin Grid Array) Pentium III on it. The Socket 370 motherboards don't carry external cache, the new Celeron for Socket 370 has 128KB on the die, and the Pentium III for socket 370 has 256KB on-board.

Socket 7, Socket 8

The Intel Pentium PRO CPU is a Socket 8 device, and cannot be mistakenly inserted in another motherboard due to its unique footprint. The Intel Pentium II represents a complete departure from the socket based design, and instead requires a proprietary Slot 1 or Slot 2 system. Intel represents this as an advancement over the "limitations" of the socket based package, AMD would disagree. Cyrix also offers a non-

Socket 7 CPU, the MediaGX series, which includes onboard sound and video controllers. The MediaGX and it's companion support chip come on a specially designed motherboard. Pentium PCs can be loosely divided into families by their CPU socket. The standard CPU socket used on the majority of Pentium motherboards is Socket 7, but some Pentium and other upgrade processors can be used on motherboards equipped with Socket 3 (486 and overdrive CPU's), Socket 4 (60 and 66MHz Intel Pentiums) or Socket 5 (some of the mid-range Pentiums). For practical reasons involving CPU voltage, clock multipliers and BIOS support, unless you have a Socket 7 motherboard with a new BIOS you'll be better off buying a new motherboard if you upgrade your CPU.

The primary manufacturers of Socket 7 CPUs are Intel, AMD and Cyrix. All offer CPUs in two classes, those compatible with the basic Pentium and an MMX (Multi Media eXtension) version. Both Cyrix and AMD include a "Performance Rating" (read Pentium Rating) with their CPUs, equating their performance with basic Intel Pentium clock rates. In the following table, the speed in MHz shown is actually the Performance rating for the Cyrix CPUs, which run at a slower clock.

Intel Pentium 60MHz to 200MHz Intel Pentium MMX 166MHz to 233 MHz

AMD-K5 PR 90MHz to 166MHz AMD K6 (with MMX) 166MHz to 266 MHz

Cyrix 6x86 133MHz to 200MHz Cyrix 6x86MX 166MHz to 266 MHz

All of these Socket 7 CPUs are designed to run Windows 95, DOS/ Windows, and the vast majority of software ever written for PCs. Some of the newest software packages which require MMX support will not run on the Intel Pentium, the AMD K5 PR, or the Cyrix 6x86, and for anybody buying new, an MMX CPU is a must. Performance for all of these CPUs is in the same ballpark at a given speed, but benchmark tests may show pretty large differences based on instruction mix and application. If you are an avid 3-D game player, this could make a big difference. If your main application is Microsoft Office, you probably won't notice.

ATX (AT eXtension) Components

For over 10 years, from about 1985 to 1997, the AT form factors established by the original IBM PC-AT provided the standard for the 90% of the PC industry. Change has finally arrived, and the majority of new systems are being built with an ATX motherboard, ATX case and ATX power supply. An ATX power supply, with suitable adapters, can be used to power an old AT style motherboard (P8 and P9 connectors), however an old case and power supply can neither power nor house a new ATX motherboard. The ATX specification was generated by Intel, but is freely distributed and is rapidly becoming the default standard for the future.

ATX Motherboards

The ATX motherboard form factor corrects some long standing problems of the original AT and baby AT designs from the purely mechanical point of view. On most AT motherboard designs, the CPU was placed behind the adapter slots, towards the front of the case, often blocking as many as three of these slots from using full length adapter cards. Also, the cooling airflow provided by the power supply exhaust fan was blocked and baffled by the adapter cards, drive cages and ribbon cables. On ATX motherboards, the CPU is mounted within inches of the fan intake, allowing for passive cooling on with some of the lower heat producing CPUs. The ATX specification has already been supplemented with the micro-ATX version, which provides for a lower cost, somewhat limited implementation for the inexpensive consumer market PC.

ATX motherboards eliminate the tangle of cables running from onboard controllers to ports on the back of the case by integrating these ports on the back edge of the motherboard. Standard features on all ATX motherboards include PS/2 style mouse and keyboard connectors, two serial ports, one enhanced parallel (printer) port, a game port and a USB (Universal Serial Bus) port. More highly integrated motherboards can include sound jacks (microphone, speakers, line in), modem ports (a line in and phone jack), RJ-45 ports (10Base-T twisted pair networking), a VGA connector and even a composite video (S Video) jack. ATX motherboards are available for older Socket 7 CPUs (the original Pentium and Pentium MMX generations), and are practically the exclusive choice for newer Pentium II and Celeron CPUs.

ATX Case

The standard ATX Case, whether a desktop, minitower or full tower, has two fundamental design changes from the AT style cases. First, it provides the proper geometry for mounting the ATX motherboard and power supply via screws and stand-off. Second, it provides a double height (enough room for two stacked ports) aperture along a length of the motherboard at the back of the case to expose all of the on-board ports and connectors. Outside of that, it's pretty much the same assembly of sheet metal and plastic that characterized the AT cases, the cheapest ones will still sport burrs to slice unwitting fingers.

ATX Power Supply

The ATX Power supply exchanges the two, 6 wire leads P8 and P9 leads of the AT power supply for a single 20 wire connector. The new additions, in terms of voltages and signals, are three+3.3V leads and a PS-ON (Power Supply On) signal, by which the power supply can be shut off or on. The drive connectors remain the same as with the AT supply, a combination of 4-lead mini-drive and drive connectors, providing+12 (Yellow) and+5 (Red) Volts, separated by two grounds. As with all switching power supplies, a minimum load is required for the supply to become active, i.e. either the motherboard or a drive must be connected. The 20 pin connector employs two rows of ten as follows (Note: Pin 1 hole is keyed as square)

Pin # Signal Signal Pin #

11 3.3 V 3.3 V 1

12-12 V 3.3 V 2

13 Ground Ground 3

14 PS-ON 5 V 4

15 Ground Ground 5

16 Ground 5 V 6

17 Ground Ground 7

18-5 V PW-OK 8

19 5 V 5V SB 9

20 5 V 12 V 10

New CPU features

The latest CPU designs are all Superscalar and Super pipelined. Superscalar architecture provides two pipelines for executing multiple instructions in parallel. Super pipelining improves data flow by increasing the number of pipeline stages, allowing for results from either pipeline to be simultaneously used to avoid stalls, a technique know as Removing Data Dependency. Out-of-order processing allows instructions in one pipeline to finish processing before a previous instruction in the other pipeline completes. Register renaming gives the CPU dynamic control of register data without having to refer to cache or main memory. Multiple Branch Prediction lets the CPU pre-fetch possible next instructions to rather than waiting for the outcome and Speculative Execution of instructions can lead to the most probable path. Internal cache size has reached 64KB on some CPUs, and unified cache holds instructions and data in any ratio which increases the hit rate from separate data and instruction caches of equal size. Dual voltage CPUs run the processor core at a lower voltage than the standard 3.3V required on the I/O pins for compatibility with CMOS circuitry. All of the CPUs discussed here are fully x86 binary code compatible, all but the first generation support industry-standard MMX(TM) instructions.

CPU Specifics

Intel P4

The Intel P4 is a higher clock speed processor than the Athlon, and is paired with Rambus RIMM memory for super low latency memory transfers. However, due to the current lack of optimized software and bandwidth issues, lower clock speed Athlon paired with 266MHz DDR memory can handily outperform P4's in many high demand applications, i.e. games. The P4 was originally available as a Socket 423 processor (no slot version) and Intel is introducing a more flexible Socket 478 platform in the Fall of 2001.

AMD Athlon

The Athlon is serious competition for Intel's Pentium 4, and actually beats the Pentium III's performance, depending on the benchmark used. Athlon based systems will only become faster when AMD releases a new chipset in mid-2000 that supports DDR to take full advantage of the Athlon 200MHz front side bus, which will also be available in a 266MHz version. The original Athlon was a Slot A processor, which looks very similar to Intel's Slot 1 and Slot 2 CPUs, but the notch is on the opposite side. AMD is phasing out the Slot A Athlon in favor of the Socket A version.

Intel Pentium III

Pentium III is Intel's most advanced CPU which is the fifth major CPU in Intel's P6 architecture line. P6 began with the Pentium PRO (as some of you who have installed a Celeron and seen it reported by the BIOS as a Pentium PRO may have noticed), that continued with the Pentium II, Celeron (all versions), and Pentium II Xeon. Pentium III CPUs are currently available as Slot 1 devices and at the slower speeds as Socket 370 chips. Some motherboards designed before Pentium III's release, such as Intel's SE440BX, can fully support the Pentium III with a Flash BIOS upgrade. I can't comment about support on other older Slot 1 motherboards, except to say that at the current price points, it doesn't make much sense to try.

AMD Duron

The AMD Duron is to the AMD Athlon what the Intel Celeron is to the Intel Pentium III, i.e., the "lite" version. The CPU core technology is the same as the Athlon. I'd be willing to bet that performance will fall in the same ballpark as the Pentium III/Celeron divide. The Duron is available in Slot A and Socket A.

Intel Pentium II

The Pentium II incorporates the best features of the Pentium MMX and the Pentium PRO in a single chip. Performance enhancing features include: 64 bit Dual Independent Bus architecture (system bus & cache bus), "glueless" support for dual Pentium II processors enabling simplified 2-way symmetric multiprocessing capable of handling 64GB of RAM, onboard 16K instruction and 16K data l caches, 7.5 million transistors in 0.25: technology for increased speed and lower power consumption, Pentium7 Pro Processor's Dynamic Execution Technology (see Pentium PRO). The independent cache bus runs at half the CPU clock, giving a bus speed of 166MHz with a 333MHz processor, compared with the 66MHz bus speed of current Socket 7 CPUs. The Pentium II is packaged in a Single Edge Contact (S.E.C.) cartridge which requires a motherboard supporting Slot 1 or Slot 2 CPU connector(s). The Pentium II is currently available in CPU speeds from 200MHz to 400MHz.

Intel Celeron

The new Celeron CPUs come with 128KB of onboard cache, and are available both for Slot 1 and for Socket 370, a new architecture specifically designed for lower cost Celeron systems. The original Celeron processor was a 266MHz CPU intended to compete in the low cost PC market. The Celeron is based on the Pentium II (P6) core, with 7.5 Million transistors in 0.25: technology, 32 KB of combined Level 1 (onboard) cache, full MMX compatibility and Dynamic Execution support (see Pentium PRO).

Intel Pentium PRO

One of the new features introduced with this CPU is Intel's Pentium7 Pro Processor's Dynamic Execution Technology which predicts the program flow through multiple branches, speeding the eventual execution of the proper instructions. The technology can actually change the order of executed instructions based on analyzed data dependencies for optimum execution speed. Since Superscalar CPUs have the ability to execute more than one integer instruction simultaneously, instructions may be carried out instructions speculatively to make the best possible use of the available computing power. The Pentium PRO is only available in speeds from 150MHz to 200MHz and has 16KB of internal cache, compared with the 32KB of the Pentium II and Pentium MMX cores..

Intel Pentium MMX

The Pentium MMX contains 4.5 million transistors a 0.35: technology. It has double the Level 1 instruction and data cache of the original Pentium and the Pentium PRO CPUs, for a total 32KB internal cache. According to Intel, the MMX's multimedia performance is more than 60% faster than an original Pentium running at the same clock speed, thanks in part to the integrated the SIMD technology (Single Instruction, Multiple Data). Intel's MMX technology includes 57 new instructions, 4 new data types and eight 64-bit wide MMX technology registers. The CPU is available in speeds from 166MHz to 333MHz, and has roughly the same cooling requirements as an older Pentium of the same speed.

Intel Pentium (R)

The Pentium processor was the first of the Intel CPUs to employ a Superscalar architecture which can execute two instructions per clock cycle. This results in up to two times the integer performance relative of an Intel 486 CPU running at the same frequency. The FPU (Floating Point Unit or Math Coprocessor) can execute two floating-point instructions in a single clock, and with pipelining (instruction scheduling and overlap) may achieve over five times the floating-point performance of a

Similar clocked 486 CPU. The CPU also introduces on-chip dual-processing support to simplify multiprocessor motherboard and software design, and an onboard interrupt controller. The Pentium processor has 3.3 million transistors, was designed for Socket 5/7, and was manufactured in speeds from 75 to 200MHz (the 60 and 66MHz models were a sort of intermediate CPU, and were Socket 4 devices)

AMD K6-3

The K6-3 is AMD's newest CPU in their K6 line, currently available at 450MHz, so giving Intel CPUs a run for their money. With 256KB of onboard cache, it's not just for breakfast anymore. The K6-3 is CPU, requires a Super 7 motherboard to take full advantage of its 100MHz L3 cache capability. Sticking it on an old Socket 7 motherboard and fooling with the multiplier jumpers to try to get it to work may be risky. I've received lots of mail lately from Socket 7 over clockers reporting permanent CPU damage, and I suspect that the day of the "seat of the pants" stuff is coming to a close.

AMD K6-2

This is the CPU that put AMD back on the map, with its 3D now enhanced instruction set; it became a favorite with gamers, and actually outperformed Intel CPUs in some applications. The K6-2 is a Socket 7 CPU, but its newest versions run at much faster clock rates than the older Socket 7 boards can support, so direct CPU upgrades aren't always possible. The overall story on the K6-2 is that it's a great CPU, but don't over clock it.

AMD K6

The AMD K6 is a RISC (Reduced Instruction Set Computing) CPU that offers full compatibility with the x86 instruction set, including MMX instructions. AMD is betting on the industry standard philosophy, and have focused their design efforts into maintaining performance par with Intel and Cyrix while retaining full Socket 7 compatibility. The advanced RISC design includes seven parallel execution units, two level branch prediction, speculative execution, full out-of-order execution, data forwarding and register renaming. The 64KB on chip L1 cache is divided into dual ported 32KB instruction and data caches. The K6's branch prediction is implemented in an 8,192-entry branch history table, a branch target cache, and a return address stack, for which AMD claims a combined prediction rate better than 95 percent. The K6 CPU is fabricated as 8.8 million transistors in 0.25: technology and is currently available in speeds up to 300MHz.

AMD K5 PRxx

The K5-PRxx was the first of AMDs CPUs to be fully implemented in RISC, capable operating on four instructions per clock cycle or twice as many as the dual pipelined Pentium. The K5 is pin compatible with the Pentium (Socket 7), and the "P-rating" gives the equivalent performance relative to Pentium CPUs. The K5 PRxx was manufactured in "P" ratings from 90 MHz to 166MHz.

Cyrix MediaGX

The MediaGX is the most highly integrated CPU system available yet, approaching a "PC on a chip", or two chips, in this case. Cyrix has implemented much of the functionality of PC adapters in firmware (they call it Virtual System Architecture), and the CPU also includes support for two USB (Universal Serial Bus) ports, MPEG1 decoding, and the required MMX support. The CPU includes three new innovations, trademarked by Cyrix as XpressRAM, XpressGRAPHICS, and XpressAUDIO. With XpressRAM, the memory controller is placed on the chip, allowing direct access to SDRAM and eliminating the need for external cache. XpressGRAPHICS replaces the graphics adapter. And dynamically configures the inexpensive main system RAM for use as video memory. XpressAUDIO replaces the sound card. The MediaGX CPU requires a special motherboard, and is particularly well suited to notebook PCs, which are all proprietary anyway.

Cyrix MII

The M II is a Socket 7 CPU, dual-voltage CPU, with the core running at 2.9V and the I/O bus at 3.3V. The MII is based on the 6x 86 cores with complete MMX instructions, enhanced memory management unit and a 64-KB internal cache. Cyrix reports the performance benchmarks of the MII 300 as equivalent of the Pentium II 300MHz.

Cyrix 6x86 MMX

The 6x86MX CPU is fully MMX compatible, includes 64KB of internal RAM and a scratchpad RAM feature. It employs a Super pipelined, Superscalar design for executing multiple instructions in one clock cycle, out of order execution, speculative execution and data dependency reduction. The 6x86 is Socket 7 compatible, and was positioned as an alternative to the Intel Pentium MMX, with relative performance ratings from 166MHz to 266MHz.

Cyrix 6x86

The 6x86 was competitive with the original Intel Pentium. It included 16KB dual ported unified cache, a 256 entry branch target buffer, and an integrated FPU (Floating Point Unit). The original 6x86 is out of production and hard to find.

Cache Memory

Once data is brought to the CPU and stored in the internal cache it can be crunched away at the basic clock speed of the chip, somewhere between 133MHz and 333MHz for most Pentium generation computers. However, the amount of internal cache on the CPU, between 32KB and 64KB of combined data and instruction cache is many orders of magnitude below the size of the average program (Megabytes) or average hard drive (Gigabytes). The internal cache is supplemented by secondary or L2 (Level 2) cache on Pentium system, normally about 512KB. Often called external cache, the secondary cache system employs SRAM (Static Ram) which 4 or 5 times faster than DRAM and doesn't require refreshing and all of the overhead that incurs. It's also many times more expensive than DRAM, which explains its limited use in PCs.

The Memory Bus

The memory bus gives the CPU access to the main memory, somewhere between 64MB and 256MB on the average new system. The speed of this bus remained constant at 66MHz from the time the fast 486 CPU's came out, around 1993, until PC100/133 memory was introduced 5 or 6 years later. The main reason for this was that the DRAM used in main memory couldn't be run any faster, and generally requires wait states (time-outs) to work with the CPU even at the 66MHz bus speed. A 100MHz memory bus designed to work with SDRAM (Synchronous DRAM) came into use on some Socket 7 motherboards and the Slot 1/Slot 2 systems. The PC100/133 SDRAM is currently being replaced by Double Data Rate DDR SDRAM at speeds of 200/266MHz. The key here is motherboard support, stuffing some expensive DDR RAM in your old motherboard, even if it supported SDRAM at 133MHz, won't get you any increased performance.

Memory Types

DRAM has been used in PCs since they first appeared in the early Eighties. The main attractions of DRAM are the lower unit cost and power consumption, it's slower and more complicated to use than above mentioned SRAM which was actually invented first. DRAM takes advantage of a peculiarity of transistor physics to temporarily store a capacitate charge (your data bit) on one of the transistors leads. Since this charge dissipates in a matter of milliseconds, the data bit must be re-read and recharged every couple hundredths of a second. This refreshing process is carried on by a dedicated controller, but the overhead involved carries a performance penalty. Today's DRAM is about 5 time faster the that used in the original PC, and the one bit wide 64KB DIP (Dual Inline Package) chip has given way to the 72 bit wide 64MB DIMM (Dual Inline Memory Module).

FPM (Fast Page Memory) was the first big performance enhancement to DRAM, which previously treated each memory bank transaction like re-inventing the wheel. FPM makes it faster to access data in the same memory "page" though the term "row" offers a better representation of what actually goes on. When a new data bit is to come from the same row as the previous bit, the memory controller need only increment the column location, and the same row address will be used, saving a transaction.

EDO Extended Data Out) DRAM shortens the recovery time between sequential RAM reads, offering up to a 20% performance boost in overall memory throughput. EDO is backwards compatible, meaning in most cases it will function in systems that only support FPM RAM, but there will be no performance gain unless the motherboard and BIOS specifically support EDO access. BEDO (Burst EDO) is the next level of performance in which a series, or burst of bytes from memory are transferred to the CPU with a single request. If the CPU actually requires the next sequential memory address in the following fetch, an operation has been saved.

SDRAM (Synchronous DRAM) can really boost memory bandwidth through synchronizing itself with the system clock. This eliminates the vast majority of timing delays which can result in wait states being taken by the CPU. The motherboard and BIOS must be designed for SDRAM for it to be installed. You may have to set the SIMM slot voltage on the motherboard with a jumper to either 5V or 3.3V.

DDR (Double Data Rate) SDRAM is currently being sampled and should be commercially available by mid-2000. Like the name implies, it doubles the effective throughput of current SDRAM modules by transferring data on both the rising and falling clock. This leads to effective speeds throughputs of 2.1GB/s and 1.6GB/s, which will be known as PC2100 and PC1600 DDR. All this just in time for operation with AMDs new chipsets for the Athlons 200MHz and 266MHz front-side bus.

RAMBUS RIMM-I still have some studying up to do on this. Basically, it's a proprietary technology that produce by a company of the same name, that Intel has started using on some high end motherboards. The modules are very expensive, and can achieve data rates as high as 800MHz, but it's a serial scheme, and I read somewhere that they only use 16 lines for the bus, leading to the same throughput as a 64 bit bus (standard) running at 200MHz (soon to come).

Parity and ECC RAM

Two different methods are in common use for catching errors in RAM; they are also used to monitor data integrity on all sorts of bus transfers within your computer or serial transfers over your modem. Parity is a relatively straight-forward system in which an extra parity bit is added to each byte, and this bit is set to 0 or 1 depending on whether the numbers of set bits in the data byte are even or odd. However, in the case of a failed parity check, the memory controller has no determining which bit was wrong, so it can only ask that the data be retransmitted, or halt the system with a parity error. Also, if two bits in the same byte with different values flip, the parity check will report no error, since the byte comparison value remains even or odd. Many PCs that use parity memory include an option in CMOS to turn off parity checking, and will work with SIMMs that lack the extra parity bit.

Error Correction Code (ECC) memory, as the name implies, is capable of actually correcting single bit errors on the fly, and catching multiple bit errors. Since this requires more extra bits per byte and extra data lines back to the memory controller, ECC RAM is more expensive to manufacture and implement. However, with memory prices falling so rapidly, ECC RAM has become much more affordable and is no longer used exclusively in servers or engineering workstations. A new development called EOS (ECC Onboard SIMM) simplifies the motherboard circuitry but is overkill for the average home PC.

For more than you want to know about memory, visit Kingston-Memory.

Drive Basics

Hard drives are still faster in every way than optical drives, including CD-ROM and DVD. The two main figures of merit for any drive with spinning media are it's random access time (in milliseconds), which describes how long it takes the drive to get the read head positioned over the location of your data, and the maximum transfer rate, which is a measure how fast (in Megabytes/second) the drive can make data available to the controller. Most drives come with a small onboard cache, works two ways. If the drive is slower than the interface speed, as is usually the case, the cache can be quickly filled and the CPU can go on to do other things while the hard drive or CDR (CD Recorder) writes the information to disk. A minimum of 1MB of cache is particularly important in the case of CDRs, since they cannot be interrupted in the course of a write session, or the disc is ruined. In the case of a super fast drive running on a slow interface, or reading while the CPU is busy doing something else, the cache acts as a temporary storage place for the data. Controllers and drives using advanced DMA (Direct Memory Access) modes avoid the latter problem, since the CPU is out of the transfer loop.

New hard drives are generally categorized by their spindle speed (rotational rate) and their interface. The maximum transfer rates of the newest EIDE and SCSI interfaces so outstrip the drives maximum physical transfer rate, which you're often paying for prestige rather than performance. The average access time of new hard drives is well under 10mS, the emphasis placed on this figure of merit has lessened as improvements have slowed. CD-ROMs, on the other hand, are now reaching average access times in the 70mS area, an improvement of about 5 times over as many years. The transfer rates on CDs, expressed as a multiple of the original 150KB/s transfer rate of a music CD drive, have now gone past 32X, or 4.8MB/s.

Drive Interfaces and Performance-IDE and SCSI

IDE (Intelligent or Independent Drive Electronics) won the battle for the PC hard drive back in 1992, rendering all other standards except for SCSI (Small Computer System Interface) obsolete. SCSI was able to hang around due in part to its greater flexibility in high-end computers (up to seven drives or devices could be attached to a controller and greater data rates were possible), and partly because the Apple Macintosh used SCSI devices exclusively, which created a market outlet. Even today, if you're building a PC for anything other than a network server or a high-end workstation, you'll want to uses the EIDE (Enhanced or Extended IDE) support built into the motherboard. In the case of newest EIDE and SCSI interfaces, the current generation of hard drives doesn't even come close to using the full potential of the interface; the drives simply can't transfer data fast enough. However, with EIDE, both hard drives and CD-ROMs are cheaper, and the controller interface is free, built right into the motherboard. There are other ways of connecting drives to a system: an Enhanced Printer Port (EPP), also known as an Extended Capability Port (ECP), is often used for connecting removable media drives or inexpensive scanners; large computers often employ serial Fiber Optic busses.

IDE, ATA, ATA-2, ATA-3, ATA-4, ATAPI, Fast-ATA, EIDE, Ultra ATA/33,/66,/100

The original IDE interface was defined by the ATA (AT Attachment, as in PC-AT) standard, adopted by ANSI, and amounted to little more than some buffering between the system I/O bus and the IDE drive, which has a controller onboard. The two drive interface did allow for a secondary channel, which would take another interrupt and additional address space. So, IDE and ATA refer to the same thing, and numbered versions of ATA refer to subsequent enhancements of the standard. ATAPI is a major upgrade, the ATA Packet Interface, which extends the ability of the interface to work with CDs, DVDs and tape drives. The EIDE, which I use somewhat generically (and incorrectly) is actually a Western Digital Trademark for their ATA implementation, Fast-ATA was coined by Seagate, both support PIO mode 3 or better and DMA mode 1 or better (see table below). Ultra ATA/100 is the newest DMA tricks, not yet incorporated in ATA standards.

EIDE Basics

The EIDE interface supports up to four drives, a Master and Slave on each of two channels. Both the interface and the EIDE drives are built with varying capabilities, though backwards compatibility can usually be taken for granted. The basic, no frills or special BIOS support speed of the IDE or ATA interface is around 3.3 MB/s (megabytes/second). This is good enough to keep up with a 22X CD-ROM, or most hard drives with the old 3600 RPM spindle speed (3600 disc revolutions per minute). The intermediate PIO (Programmed or Processor I/O) modes and DMA (Direct Memory Access) modes used by EIDE and Fast-ATA are big performance boosters, the highest are somewhat vaporware-like, the drives that can produce these transfer rates don't exist. There are five possible PIO modes and three DMA modes, shown in the table. For more than you want to know about EIDE, visit the ATA FAQ-IDE interface.

PIO Mode 0 PIO Mode 1 PIO Mode 3 PIO Mode 4 PIO Mode 5

3.3MB/s 5.2MB/s 8.3MB/s 11.1MB/s 16.6MB/s

DMA Mode 1 DMA Mode 2 Ultra DMA UDMA/66 UDMA/100

13.3MB/s 16.6MB/s 33MB/s 66MB/s 100MB.s

The main thing to know about IDE hard drives is for speeds above 66MB/s (all new hard drives) you need to use an 80 conductor IDE cable.

SCSI Interface and Drives

The SCSI (Small Computer Systems Interface) is actually the oldest (and still champion) standard in use for connecting drives and high performance peripherals to PCs. With the exception of the cheapest SCSI throw-away adapters sometimes shipped with proprietary CDs or scanners, all SCSI adapters support up to 7 devices (14 for SCSI-2), in any combination including those internal and external to the system box. SCSI devices all remain backward compatible, you should be able to attach the newest devices to your oldest controller, though you'll lose any performance benefits that would have been do to the higher SCSI support of the device, and you made need some pretty funky cables. The SCSI bus is inherently more reliable than the IDE interface, due in part to the large number of grounds used in SCSI cables which provide protection against electrical noise. SCSI devices that are commonly available in both internal and external versions include: hard drives, tape backups, CD-ROMs, CDRs (CD Recorders) and optical drives. The most common external-only SCSI peripheral is the scanner, though cheaper scanners are increasingly relying on the enhanced printer port.

Level Known As Number of Devices Max. Transfer Speed Bus Width

SCSI-1 SCSI 7 (8 includes controller) 5 MB/S 8 bits

SCSI-2 Fast SCSI 7 10 MB/S 8 bits

Fast Wide SCSI 15 (16 includes controller) 20 MB/s 16 bits

SCSI-3 Ultra SCSI 7 20MB/S 8 bits

Ultra Wide SCSI 15 40MB/S 16 bits

Ultra-2 SCSI 7 40MB/S 8 bits

Ultra-2 Wide SCSI 15 80MB/S 16 bits

Ultra-3 SCSI 7 80MB/S 8 bits

Ultra-3 Wide SCSI 15 160MB/S 16 bits

SCSI devices are usually among the most simple to install, with termination being the sole wild card. SCSI devices require termination at both ends of the bus to absorb which untenanted power, which prevents reflections of the radio frequency signals within the transmission line. The SCSI adapter is found in the middle of the bus, when both internal and external devices are devices come with either resistor packs to be removed for an exterminated device (old style) or asingle jumper on newer devices. External SCSI devices may provide a switch for termination, but more commonly they require installation of a snap on terminator on the outgoing side of daisy chained port. Some SCSI devices are available in the "differential bus" bus flavor, which further increases noise immunity and allow longer distances for external devices, but these cannot be mixed with standard SCSI devices and follow their own termination rules. For more than you want to know about SCSI, visit Adaptec-SCSI.

56K Modems-USR x2, k56flex and V.90

There is no reason today to put anything other than a 56K modem in a new PC. This doesn't guarantee that you'll get anywhere near 56K when you connect, but given the prices and the probability that your ISP (Internet Service Provider) will upgrade in the near future, an old V.34 (33K) modem is a waste of money. There are currently 3 standards for 56K modems, and which are implemented in software (firmware) both on your modem and at the ISP. The original x2 standard introduced by US. Robotics (acquired by 3COM) and the k56flex standard from Rockwell and Lucent are NOT compatible with each other, nor with the V.90 standard which replaces them. However, since these standards exist in firmware (the hardware is inter-operable), these modems are almost always software upgradeable to the V.90 standard. However, unless the modem has sufficient onboard flash memory (EEPROM) to hold the code for both it's original standard and the new V.90 standard, you may lose one when you switch to the other. All of this is particularly important because of the long shelf life of modems in stores, and the future availability of bargains if you don't mind taking a few minutes to do the firmware upgrade.

How it Works

There are several limitations on what speed you can actually expect out of your 56K modem, not the least of these being the FCC which limits transmissions to 53K by law. In order for you to reach 56K on downloads, you need to be calling an ISP or other source with a true digital modem. In all point-to-point calls, the central phone office, where the calls are actually switched, stands in between. The phone company networks are all digital, allowing for clean, high speed transfers between switching points, and for 56K to work, your ISP must be digitally connected to that network. The 56K modem in your PC is strictly an analog device, so an A/D conversion is done at the central office on your upstream data, and a D/A conversion is done on your downstream data (downloads). As it happens, the line noise that had modem speeds limited to 33K is largely caused by A/D conversion, which is why your upstream speed is still limited to 33K. Since the all-digital connection between the ISP and the central office eliminates the A/D conversion on the downstream link, speed up to 56K become possible. However, if there are other noise sources involved, due to poor house-to-central office wiring, you may never reach these speeds. In fact, if your 28K modem rarely connects at the full 28K, you're going to be disappointed.

DVD Drives and Technology

Much like CD-ROM before it, DVD has come to the computer industry by way of the entertainment industry. CDs were originally designed for the music industry, and over the course of a decade replaced the old LPs. CDs didn't begin a new life as data storage devices for computers until long after they were an established winner in home audio. DVDs are designed (primarily) as a higher quality, harder to pirate replacement for the VHS tapes and Laser Discs currently used to distribute movies. Unlike CDs, DVDs are expected to have their greatest initial success as data storage devices for PCs, and replace VCRs only gradually. Part of the reason is cost, another factor is that, their is currently no reasonable way for homeowners to record television shows on DVD.

The technology of DVDs is very similar to that of CDs, and for the time being, CDs are actually faster than DVDs. A dual speed DVD has a native data transfer rate of approximately an 18X CD, the single speed DVD data rate is equivalent to a 9X CD. DVD players for computers are available in EIDE (ATAPI) and SCSI flavors, starting around $250. To play back DVD movies in your PC, you'll either need some extra hardware for decoding MPEG-2 and handling the special audio tracks, or a fast enough CPU (at least a 233MHz MMX) to do the job. DVDs capacity is about 4.7GB per layer per side, with one or two layers per side for a maximum of around 18GB. Two sided discs must be ejected and turned over manually. All DVD players can read manufactured CD-ROMs, many have problems with CDR discs. There are two types of DVD recorders available for PCs, DVD-RAM and DVDR, both are good for recording data, not movies, and they fall short of 4GB per side. Various copy protection schemes may make future DVD movie discs unviewable in some current drives. A DVD Audio standard is not yet finalized, and will probably be very slow to catch on, given the good quality and current installed based of CD stereos. For more than you want to know about DVD, visit The DVD FAQ.

The Video Subsystem

The video monitor is generally the most expensive single component of a basic PC system, which isn't a bad thing since it's also the only component comes close to holding it's value over time. A monitor is very similar to an artists canvas, in that it presents no images or information on it's own, it needs to be painted by a remote hand or controller. The video adapter installed in your PC may only cost around 10% as much as the monitor, but it's the adapter that controls the resolution of the image and the number of colors displayed. Certainly, there are trade-offs between the two, you can buy very expensive video adapters intended for rapidly rendering high-resolution 3D graphics in a flicker free display, and these require a monitor capable of handling the high data transfer speed.

Monitor Electronics

Since information is actually passed from the video adapter to the monitor in analog form, i.e. varying voltage levels to describe the intensity for the Red, Green, and Blue electron guns, plus some synchronization signals, the transfer rate ends up being described in terms of refresh frequencies. The monitor electronics steer the beams from these electron guns by use of magnetic fields (also called lenses), which deflect the beams down and across the screen at speeds determined by the vertical and horizontal refresh frequencies. The vertical refresh rate describes how many times the entire screen is redrawn in a second, and the horizontal frequency must be fast enough to steer the beam all the way across the screen enough times to paint every pixel in a single vertical scan.

Pixels are a description of image resolution, with no particular dependence on the monitor used, as long as the monitor electronics can keep up with the high scan rates needed if a lot of pixels need to get painted in a single vertical pass, and a lot of vertical passes (say 75 to 85) are desired each second for a really stable picture. The sharpness of the images painted, however, is dependent on the dot-pitch, or stripe-pitch of the monitor phosphor. The pitch is a measure, in millimeters, of the distance between two phosphor dots or stripes of the same color on the inside surface of the monitor screen. Some manufacturers use a aperture or mask pitch measurement which actually describes the size of the holes in part of the beam focusing train, but an equivalent phosphor dot-pitch measurement should be available. Actual dot pitch sizes still in use (forget about the bad old days) runs from about .25mm to .31mm, all of which look good to me.

What all this means to the average computer owner is that very little has changed in the past five years or so, except that interlaced monitors (those that painted only a half a screen at a time, skipping every other line each vertical scan to reduce flicker) have been phased out, and many new video cards no longer support the slowest VGA compatibility modes these monitors used. In other words, if you try hooking your monitor from 1992 or 1993 on your new AGP graphics cards, it may not work. Monitors have slowly gotten cheaper, so that the 14" standard is now often sale priced below $150, and the entry level 17" monitors start around $300.

The main difficulty that most people encounter in their video subsystem is in the wrong resolution/color driver being selected for a given software application. Almost all video cards installed in systems today feature 2MB of video memory, which is enough to display 24bit True Color (16.7 Million colors) at the 800X600 resolution, the highest you'll normally want to run on a 14" or 15" screen. However, the default choice for most video drivers on installation is still 256 colors, go figure. In Windows 95/98, this is easily changed in Control Panel>Monitor, or by clicking on the little monitor in the tray at the bottom right corner of the screen.

Resolution Number of Pixels Video Ram Required for True Color

(24 bit uses 3 bytes/pixel for 16.7 Million colors)

Suggested Monitor Size

640x480 307,200 1MB 14" to 17"

800x600 480,000 2MB 14" to 17"

1024x768 786,432 4MB (3MB not commonly sold) 17" to 21"

1152x870 1002240 4MB 17" to 21"

1600x1200 1920000 8MB (6MB not commonly sold) 19" or larger

AGP and PCI Video Cards

When it comes to modern video adapters, the only real choice is whether to go with PCI or AGP. Basically, if your motherboard has an AGP slot, it's seems silly not to use it. The price difference is minor, and the pipelining supported on the AGP bus can supposedly quadruple the data transfer rate. In terms of refresh rates, resolution and #of colors, there's no difference between AGP and other graphics cards. People who upgrade motherboard in older systems sometimes hang onto their ISA Video adapter and old monitor, since the performance bottleneck for most applications were never in the video subsystem anyway.

If your motherboard has a build in video chip and you want to add a video card. You will need to do this first. Make sure you have an unused PCI slot. Buy a PCI video card they all are pretty good these days. Just make sure you have at lest 64 MB of on board RAM [64 MB of memory on the video card]. Then you will need to disable the on board video chip. This can be done in most computers Bio, most no all. To do this in most cases hold the "Delete" key when the computer first starts up.

If this does not get you into your computer's bio. You will need to look in the booklet that came with your computer to get in to the bio. Now for the people who computer's bio will not let you disable the on board video chip you my have to move come of your PCI cards around. Because if you install your new PCI video card any place but the number one slot it will not work. And the number one slot is always the slot that is the closest to your power supply. I like to install all PCI video cards in the number one slot. I find I have less problems get it to work right in the number one slot you my also.

29

How to Reprogram your Computer

First you will need to make sure you have a startup disk. If not this is how to make one. You will need one empty 3 2 inch disk. How to make a start up disk. From desktop find your start button on the lower left corner of your desktop. Go to Settings then click on Control Panel. When you get to Control Panel fine Add/Remove Programs. Double click to open. Go to Startup Disk. You will need a 3 2inch disk. Put the disk in drive and click Create Disk. From there follow there follow on screen directions.

But your startup disk in a drive. You will need a windows operating systems disk. Like Windows 9X or Windows XP. You will also need to know if it is a upgrade or full install CDROM. If it is an upgrade version you will need to have the full install disk it upgrades also. For an upgrade disk of Windows XP you will need to have the full install Windows 98 disk also. With your startup disk in drive A restart on turn on your computer. When you get to the screen asking to Start with CRROM support or not. Use the down arrow button and high light Start with CRROM support,. And click ENTER. It will take a 2 or 3 minutes to finish. When it finishes you will be at a screen that looks like A:. This is a step you my skip if you want. But if you think you my have a virus I would do this. But you will lose everything on your computer. This is why it is so important to back up everything you want to save on removable disk. At A: type format C: and click ENTER, It will ask are you sure type Y click ENTER. It will take 2 or

3 minutes to finish. When it finishes it will ask if you want to enter a label. Click ENTER to resume. It will go back to A: .Then type in D:setup, it should look like A: D: setup . And click ENTER. It will tell you it needs to run ScanDisk this it OK so click ENTER. After Scan-Disk has finished the screen will have EXIT button on right bottom of screen. Use the Right Arrow to high this and click ENTER. From here on out all you have to do is follow your on screen directions. You are just 20 to 60 minutes from reprogramming you computer. If you try to reprogram without formatting and you get a starting error or it is still messed up in some way. Then start over a format this time.

Ok now to running windows for the first time. But you do not have any sound. Not to worry. You will have to install the drives for your sound card, video card, printer, scanner, and modem. To start go to your desk top and left click on My Computer the click on properties. This will open System Properties. Click on Device Manager Look for any item that is marked with a question or exclamation mark. High light these item and click on remove; this will remove the item and any files that were installed when you installed windows. After you remove all the items marked with a marked with a question or exclamation mark. You are ready to install the drive for them devicesfrom the man-ufacturer. These disks usually have step by step directions so just follow them. After you install one of these it will ask to restart your computer. After you restart some time it will ask for the manufacturer's disk again.

Most people find that installing the device drives are harder then installing the operating system. But stick with it you will get it. And you will find that each time you do this it gets a little easier.

30

Miscellaneous

Part1: Internet slang and its meanings

LOL meaning Laugh Out Loud

h4x0r' meaning hacker

'warez' meaning the illegal distribution of software

'31337' meaning elite

'omg' meaning O my God

"Rad" meaning cool

"K" means "kay" or "Kilobyte", or 1024 bytes.

'Phear' (feer) meaning action of comically being scared of something

'haus' (hows)to be "in da huas" is to have arrived, entering an area where you and your buddies hang out

'Biotch' (bee-otch) Most common spellings: Biotch, bi0tch, beeatch, bizitch meaning bitch-used as an insult or as a term of friendly rivalry

'jargon' meaning without qualifier

'techspeak 'meaning programming

'cruft' (kruhft) meaning unpleasant substance.

'ur' meaning your

'u' meaning you

Letter Replacements:

q=k, ck

0=o

ew=oo

ewe=u, you

ph=f

@, 4=a

3=e

z=s

|=I

Part2: Ink-jet printers and scanners

dpi means dots per inch. Ink-jet printer

work in dpi. So if you have 1400 X 720 dpi

printer you need a scanners that is 1400 X 720

or less. So in other words you need a matched

pair for best results.

A USB scanner is faster then a serial port scanner.

USB stands for Universal Serial Bus. You'll find

these serial ports on the back of new PCs. USB ports

are much faster than the older variety—they can

provide throughput of 12 megabits per second. You can

attach 127 devices in a star chain to a single port.

Intel created USB in response to user difficulties

with adding hardware devices to computers. With USB,

you can connect scanners, printers, keyboards, mice,

and cameras to your PC without opening the computer

case. The spec doesn't work with Windows 95 that well,

but Windows 98 has full USB support. The above image

is the USB symbol. Look for it on the back of your computer.

Two hundred fifty-six colors, 16-bit color, and 24-bit

colors are terms that describe "color depth," the number

of colors displayed on your computer screen.

Early monochrome screens displayed white, green, or amber text on a black background. Computers with those screens use a single bit per pixel to represent color. Since a bit has two possible states (1 or 0), each pixel can be in one of two states, on or off. If the pixel is "on," that means it is glowing, which shows up as white (or green or amber, depending on the screen).

256 colors

It wasn't long before people wanted more color on their screens. The next step up were screens that could display 16 different colors. This requires four bits per pixel. Four bits can represent 16 possible states because 2 to the 4th power is 16.But with only 16 colors, you still don't get a very realistic color effect.

The next step up was 8 bits per pixel, which allows 256 colors. That's about the level of color you see in business graphics. When you get to 256 colors (8-bit color), you can start making cartoons and graphics that look like drawings. Icons, for the most part, use either 16 or 256 colors.

16-bit color

The 256-color scheme is pretty good for simple graphics

but not for photo reproduction. As graphic displays on

the computer got more sophisticated, people wanted to see photos on their computers and on the Web, so they added even more bits per pixel. With 16 bits per pixel (16-bit color) you get 2 to the 16th power worth of color combinations—65,000 color combinations. That's sometimes called a high-color display and its good enough for most graphics. Most games use16-bit color.

24-bit color

It is estimated that the eye can resolve roughly 2 million

different colors and shades. To get 2 million shades, you need 24 bits of color information per dot, or 24-bit color. This is called "true color."

For almost everybody—except high-end graphic artists—24-bit color is sufficient. However, there are displays that can go to an even higher color resolution. Using 32-bit color produces over 4 billion different shades.

If you have a VGA monitor, it's your video card, not the monitor, which determines how colors you can display. Most video cards can display at least 8-bit color, and almost all can display 16-bit color (high color). If you have enough memory in your video card, you can display 24-bit color (true color) and 32-bit the highest quality setting.

Part 3: Joysticks

The best joysticks are digital joysticks.

Analog joysticks have to be polled by the CPU. That means that the CPU periodically checks the joystick for new data. This checking process sucks up about 5 to 10 percent of your processing power and reduces reaction speed. If gaming response time and CPU speed are critical, using an analog joystick can make a difference in the game's performance.

Digital joysticks don't work that way; they send their data straight to the CPU, so time and power are not wasted in the polling process.

The most common way of connecting a joystick is through the sound card's joystick port. Both analog and digital joysticks usually support this option. There are also serial-port joysticks out there, but they are usually the higher-end joysticks. USB joysticks come in both digital and analog flavors. However, analog joysticks require an analog-to-digital converter. In your case, whichever connection option your computer supports is the one you should use. That will give you the best performance for your particular joystick.

Part 4: FINDING LOST CD KEYS IN YOUR REGISTRY

You can find your lost CD key from your own registry with the steps below:

Make the CD code to unlock software reappear. You just think you lost that CD key code, which is imprinted on the software's box or in the documentation and permits you to reinstall the program.

You won't have to call a support line and wait hours for a tech to regurgitate that lost code for you, it's not really lost. Windows saved it in a cubbyhole called the Registry.

Don't play around while you go through these steps, though. Deleting some Registry files can cause massive headaches.

And it's always best to follow your manual's instructions and back up the registry before starting.

Here's the procedure:

Launch REGEDIT by selecting Start/Run, typing REGEDIT in the text box and pressing Enter.

Under HKEY_LOCAL_MACHINE, click on the+and scroll down to Software.

Find the Microsoft listing click on it, and look for the directory that contains software you need to reinstall.

Double-click the Product ID listing and select the middle two number strings. For example, in the string 53491-460-1656111-49145, you'd select 460-1656111. (for Office 97)

To find the Windows CD Key: find Windows, click the "current version" with the+sign, don't click the+sign, click on the words "current version". The product ID and the product key will appear. It's all the numbers and letters that you see.

Highlight, Press Control C to copy the CD key to the clipboard, then paste it someplace where you can reuse it. Some experts advise compiling all your keys to a text document, then printing it out for safekeeping.

Part 5: Block that spam

While looking at your inbox, go to tools, and then organize. A new panel should appear above your inbox. Click the "Junk E-Mail" tab. You need to have configured an account and downloaded mail for the tab to appear. You can choose to automatically gray-out spam messages or automatically move the messages to a certain folder. Turn the feature on. Highlight a junk mail message. Go to Actions > Junk E-mail > Add to Junk Senders List. You can also hit Alt+A, then J, then J again to add the message to junk mail without the mouse. Delete the spam message. Future messages from the sender will be treated as you specified in the third step.

Part 6: Communication Wiring Color Codes Cat 5 & 5e Network

Color Codes for RJ-45 Ethernet Plug

Eight-conductor data cable (Cat 3 or Cat 5) contains 4 pairs of wires. Each pair consists of a solid color wire and a white and color striped wire. Each of the pairs are twisted together. To maintain reliability on Ethernet, you should not untwist them any more than necessary (about 1/4 inch).

The pairs designated for 10BaseT Ethernet are orange and green. The other two pairs, brown and blue, are unused. The connections shown are specifically for an RJ45 plug. The wall jack may be wired in a different sequence because the wires may be crossed inside the jack. The jack should either come with a wiring diagram or at least designate pin numbers that you can match up to the color code below.

There are two wiring standards for these cables, called T-568A and T-568B. They differ only in pin assignments, not in uses of the various colors. The illustration above shows both standards. With the T-568B specification the orange and green pairs are located on pins 1, 2 and 3, 6 respectively. The T-568A specification reverses the orange and green connections, so that the blue and orange pairs are on the center 4 pins, which makes it more compatible with the telco voice connections.

T-568A is supposed to be the standard for new installations, and T-568B is the alternative. However, most off-the-shelf data equipment and cables seem to be wired to T568B.

Pin Number Designations

Here are the pin number designations for both standards:

T-568B

Pin Color Pair Descrtipion

1 white/orange 2 TxData+

2 orange 2 TxData-

3 white/green 3 RecvData+

4 blue 1 Unused

5 white/blue 1 Unused

6 green 3 RecvData-

7 white/brown 4 Unused

8 brown 4 Unused

T-568A

Pin Color Pair Description

1 white/green 3 RecvData+

2 green 3 RecvData-

3 white/orange 2 TxData+

4 blue 1 Unused

5 white/blue 1 Unused

6 orange 2 TxData-

7 white/brown 4 Unused

8 brown 4 Unused

Note: Odd pin numbers are always the striped wires..

Straight-Through vs Cross-Over

In general, the patch cords that you use with your Ethernet connections are "straight-through", which means that pin 1 of the plug on one end is connected to pin 1 of the plug on the other end (for either standard). The only time you cross connections in 10BaseT is when you connect two Ethernet devices directly together without a hub or connect two hubs together. Then you need a "cross-over" patch cable, which crosses the transmit and receive pairs. An easy way remember how to make a cross-over cable is to wire one end with the T-568A standard and the other with the T-568B standard.

Termination

UTP cables are terminated with standard connectors, jacks and punchdowns. The jack/plug is often referred to as a "RJ-45", but that's a telco designation for the "modular 8 pin connector" terminated with a USOC pinout used for telephones. The male connector on the end of a patchcord is called a "plug" and the receptacle on the wall outlet is a "jack."

In LANs, as spec'ed by 568, there are two possible pinouts, called T568A and T568B, that differ only in which color coded pairs are connected-pair 2 and 3 are reversed. Either work equally well, as long as you don't mix them! If you always use only one version, you're OK, but if you mix A and B in a cable run, you will get crossed pairs!

The cable pairs are color coded as

Pair 1 is white-blue/blue,

Pair 2 white-orange/orange,

Pair 3 is white-green/green

Pair 4 is white-brown/brown.

Jacks usually have punchdowns on the back or can be terminated without punchdowns using special manufacturer's tools or even a cover for the connector. Again, you MUST keep the twists as close to the receptacle as possible to minimize crosstalk.

Note that Cat 3 jacks and all plugs are going to use these color codes. However, Cat 5 jacks have internal connections that continue the twists as close to the pins in the jacks as possible. Thus the pinout on the back of the jacks will not usually follow these layouts! Always follow the color codes on the back of the jacks to insure proper connections!

Crossover Cables:

Normal cables that connect a PC/NIC card to a hub are wired straight through. That is pin 1 is connected to pin 1, pin 2 to pin 2, etc. However, if you are simply connecting two PCs together without a hub, you need to use a crossover cable made by reversing pair 2 and 3 in the cable, the two pairs used for transmisson by Ethernet. The easy way to make a crossover cable is to make one end to T568A color coding and the other end to T568B. Then the pairs will be reversed.

Punchdowns come in 4 varieties: 110, 66, Bix and Krone. Most popular for LANs is the 110 (on the left), for telcos it's the 66 (on the right), and the Bix and Krone are rare (price, proprietary designs, etc.)

110 block 66 block

Color Codes For Punchdowns:

Punchdowns of all types are always made with the pairs in order with the white/stripe wire first, then the colored wire, Pair 1(w/blue-blue), Pair 2 (w/orange-orange), Pair 3 (w/green-green), Pair 4 (w/brown-brown). (This color code is remembered by BLOG-BLueOrangeGreen and brown)

0-595-26483-2

www.ingramcontent.com/pod-product-compliance
Lightning Source LLC
Chambersburg PA
CBHW031056180526
45163CB00002BA/854